JOHN BARRINGTON is an established st[...]
750 Scottish Blackface sheep on the 2,[...]
Loch Katrine.

Successful at sheepdog trials, shepherd and dogs have given demonstration of their ancient craft at two Garden Festivals and many shows, galas and Highland Games.

In 1998, the Scottish Qualifications Authority asked John Barrington to design a course in sheepdog handling and management, which took two years to undertake. The first classes were run at Oatridge Agricultural College, near Edinburgh, in 2000, the author at the helm. Students were enrolled from Ireland, England and all parts of Scotland.

With a good eye for sheep, John Barrington has judged classes of sheep at the Royal Highland Show in Edinburgh and around Europe.

Like most shepherds, Barrington is a natural storyteller, a gift he exercises at schools, clubs and societies, and as an after dinner speaker. Stories are recounted on the move during daytime guided tours and twilight ghost walks, and as a commentator at a dozen or so Highland Games each year. Stories told to enliven his whisky tasting sessions are always presented in the right spirit! His first book, *Red Sky at Night*, was a UK bestseller and won him a Scottish Arts Council book award.

By the Same Author

Red Sky at Night (1984, new edition 2013)
Loch Lomond and the Trossachs (2006)
Out of the Mists (2008)

Of Dogs and Men

JOHN BARRINGTON
with illustrations by
BOB DEWAR

Luath Press Limited

EDINBURGH

www.luath.co.uk

To my father
who bought me my first dog.

First published 2013

ISBN: 978-1-906817-90-9

The paper used in this book is recyclable. It is made from
low chlorine pulps produced in a low energy, low emissions manner
from renewable forests.

Printed and bound by
Martins the Printers, Berwick upon Tweed

Typeset in 10.5 point Sabon
by 3btype.com

Contents

Whenever shepherds get together, humour plays a big part. Stories will be exchanged, songs sung and poems recited. I have only ever known one dog by the name of Pete, and this could be him.

A farmer's dog came into town, whose christian name was
    Pete,
His pedigree was ten yards long, his looks were hard to beat
And as he trotted down the street, 'twas beatiful to see
His work on every corner, his art on every tree.
He watered every gate and didn't miss a post,
For piddling was his masterpiece and piddling was his boast.
The city dogs stood looking on, with deep and jealous rage
To see this simple country dog, the piddler of his age.
They smell't him over one by one, they smell't him two by
    two,
The noble Pete in high disdain, stood still till they were
    through.
They sniffed him over one by one, their praise for him ran
    high,
But when one sniffed him underneath, Pete piddled in his
    eye.
Then, just to show those city dogs, he didn't give a damn,
Pete strolled into the grocer shop and piddled on the ham.
He piddled on the onions, he piddled on the floor,
And when the grocer kicked him out, Pete piddled on the
    door.
Behind him all the city dogs debated what to do,
They'd hold a piddling carnival and show the stranger
    through.
They showed him all the piddling posts they knew about the
    town.
They started out with many winks to wear the stranger
    down,

But Pete was with them every trick, with vigour and with vim
A thousand piddles more or less were all the same to him.
And on and on went noble Pete, his hind leg lifting high,
'Cause most were lifting legs in bluff and piddling mighty dry.
And on and on went noble Pete, and watered every sand hill,
Till all the city champions were piddled to a standstill.
Then Pete an exhibition gave in all the ways to piddle,
Like double-drips and fancy flips, and now and then a
    dribble.
And all this time this golden dog did neither wink or grin,
But blithely piddled out of town as he had piddled in.
The city dogs said So long, Pete. Your piddling did defeat us.
No one ever put them wise – our Pete had diabetes!

The Pete I knew was a handsome, yellow-coated dog – and did
have diabetes...

Author

This is a lovely Australian poem, by Anon.

> You can't buy loyalty, they say,
> I bought it though, the other day.
> You can't buy friendship, tried and true,
> Well, just the same, I bought that too.
>
> I bought a single, trusting heart,
> That gave devotion from the start.
> If you think these things aren't for sale,
> Buy a blue pup with a stump for a tail!

A perfect advertisement for Australian Stumpy-tail Cattle Dogs.

THIS IS SIMPLY A distillation of more than 50 years of sharing life with a succession of dogs. My parents put together the ideal family unit; me, followed by a baby sister and, at the age of ten, a very pale Golden Labrador puppy. The world for one small boy was now complete.

Family lore has it that the first cuddly toy I took to heart had been a brown dog called Whiskers. He played many roles in my young life – except as the pyjama case he was designed to be. Once my legs would adequately hold me up, my inseparable companion and I toddled off happily to explore the wonders of the Chinese Year of the Dog. One of these was the seemingly enormous German Shepherd dog belonging to my paternal grandparents, an extremely affectionate bitch called Lassie. From this early age, the love of dogs was not only flowing through my veins, it must have been fixed in my genes.

I was enthralled by any story about dogs. During the war years, my father's family owned a Wire-Haired Terrier, by the name of Flossie, who was noted for two things. Flossie had been able to fall asleep whilst standing upright and, even if sleeping, would always give a warning of an impending air raid well before the sirens sounded.

The hero of the first real book I remember reading, all words and no pictures, told the story an RAF dog called Flak. During the crucial period of World War II, Flak had flown many perilous missions with his master. I have no recollection of the name of the ace pilot, but the dog was quite a different matter.

Flak was the name bestowed on my Labrador puppy, the dog with which I soon learned all about the pleasures and responsibilities of ownership. Dogs have to be walked, even in the rain. Feeding and grooming would be rewarded with licks and slobbers, just what every schoolboy enjoys. Sadly, a few weeks before the birth of my younger sister, Flak was sent to stay with friends of the family and much to my chagrin, soon settled into his new home. At a distance of less than two miles, Flak was a frequent visitor and seemingly well taken with the new addition to our household. One night, in the early hours, baby Jane was taken ill. Even before the doctor had arrived, Flak was at the door and demanding to be let in. Inexplicably, the dog had suddenly needed to get out and must have run like the wind to make such good time from the next village. This was my first inkling of the extra sensory perception displayed by many dogs.

At Higher Hareslade Farm, pronounced as 'Haslet' in the local Gower dialect, I associated with the animals and farm dogs which were to determine my future path in life. Only little did I know it at the time. Almost at every turn I came face to face with one dog or another. The cinema and television regularly featured films starring Lassie or Rin Tin Tin. Travelling daily to and from the secondary school in Swansea, on the famous Mumbles Train, at that time the oldest passenger railway in the world, I would pass the monument to Swansea Jack. After pulling a 12-year-old boy from the oily water of the nearby docks in 1931, Jack then embarked on a six year life-saving career. The black Flat-Coated Retriever is the only dog to have been awarded two bronze medals by the National Canine Defence League. In 1936, Jack received the accolade of Bravest Dog of the Year, as well as the Lord Mayor of London's Silver Cup.

In the Swansea Jack pub, I am sure people still drink to the memory of that great dog.

Leaving grammar school at 15, before starting out on a working career I set off on a six-week hike around the near continent of Europe. In Paris, I was pointed in the direction of Asnières-sur-Seine, on the outskirts of the city. Le Cimetière des Chiens, founded in 1899, is one of the unsung wonders of the French capital. The remarkable Art Nouveau entrance alone is well worth seeing. The cemetery is home to an estimated 40,000 dead dogs, and countless living cats. A tomb has been set aside for the remains of police dogs. A monument marks the final resting place of a St Bernard called Barry der Menschenretter (1800–1814), who perished in the High Alps whilst attempting to rescue his 41st snowbound traveller. I also came upon the grave of Rin Tin Tin (1918–1932), returned from America to lie in his native soil.

Some dogs are born lucky. Rin Tin Tin was plucked out of the carnage of front-line fighting by an American serviceman in September 1918, shell-shocked and eyes not yet opened. Back in the States, a slow motion film clip of the young German Shepherd Dog, leaping 11 feet, was spotted by a Hollywood film producer – and the rest is history. Rin Tin Tin starred in 23 feature films, before dying in the arms of his co-star, the beautiful Jean Harlow. How lucky was that?

With this background of canine stories, gleaned entirely from such films, books and comics, I was about to enter into the real world of livestock and working dogs. From the start I was fortunate in my employers who, in their individual way, imparted wisdom and knowledge in equal measure. Most influential was George Ernest Rees of College Farm, Llangennith, farmer, hotelier and war-time hero. Led by Ernie Rees and Sergeant Davies, the local home guard carried out a daring rescue of two British airmen, plucked from their storm-tossed dinghy and brought up a steep cliff-face to safety. Ernie Rees was awarded the British Empire Medal by George VI. In his day a noted sportsman and athlete, it is said that Ernie gave many of the British Athletics Team a run for their money, as they trained locally for the 1936 Olympic Games. Not only did Ernie outperform several of the chosen athletes, over a range of disciplines, when asked for a training route for the middle and long distance runners, the young farmer went with them. Ernie Rees was first home. At Llangennith I was introduced to the wiles and ways of sheep, and the qualities of Welsh Black and Tan dogs.

As I worked my way steadily along my professional path, I have been well aware of the parts played by many colleagues and friends, too numerous to mention individually. However, special reference needs to be made to John Barrow in Wales, Sandy Alexander in Scotland and, more recently, to Betty Stikkers and Piet van Geest in the Netherlands. Not only did I have the benefit of working alongside many of the unnamed, a few were fellow competitors at sheepdog trials, whilst others were sometimes encountered on the running track or rugby pitches. Whatever the occasion, at some point, tales of dogs, past and present, would unfold. One thing that is certain, the longer any dog has been dead the better it gets!

From time to time, dogs become entangled in acts of downright skulduggery. One had been sent away to be trained and was reported to have died, only to be spotted many miles from home, alive and well and running at a sheepdog trial. Another missing dog was recognised by a delivery driver, on a farm at the other end of the country. Both dogs were returned to their rightful owners. Less blatant were the actions of a top sheepdog handler of a bygone age, who simply bought any dog that had the potential to challenge his supremacy on the trial field. This man was also known to have purchased an unheralded sheepdog, only he could see any potential in the animal. It was this innate ability to pick out the right sort of dog which kept him at the pinnacle of trialling for many years.

There is certainly one present day shepherdess, living and working in Northumberland, who has a similar eye for a decent working dog. At the tender age of 14, Emma Gray came across a farm collie called Bill, severely unkempt and destined for an early grave. The owner claimed that the dog had no work in him, the young lass believed differently. Once Emma's parents had been talked round, Bill found himself with a new home – and developed into a first rate sheepdog. Twenty-first century flockmasters and shepherds are a very hi tech breed, equipped with electronic gadgetry and getting around on a quad bike. They are also required to take charge of a far greater number of sheep. The one common denominator is the collie dog, every bit as important today as it has been throughout history.

Having reached retirement age, my hill boots stuffed with newspaper and the cromach hanging idly at the back of the door, I have much to be grateful for and so many people to thank. As well as to my past employers and fellow workers, my gratitude extends to a number of organisations. Under the auspices of the Scottish Development Agency, I was part of the team telling the entire story of wool during Scottish Week at the Stoke-on-Trent Garden Festival, in July 1986. Two years later, at the Glasgow Garden Festival, Edinburgh Woollen Mills sponsored the gold medal winning 'Story of Scottish Wool', which attracted over a million visitors to our site. On a more personal level, I am indebted to Subaru UK, who supported the John Barrington Sheepdog Demonstration Team and duly emblazoned a succession of cars. The committee of the Royal Highland Show also played their part, inviting me to judge the Shetland Sheep classes at Edinburgh, in 1994.

As a definite dog-and-stick man, I have relied heavily on Peter Nichols for all technical support. Luath Press have not just published my books, they were responsible for a city centre Dog and Duck demonstration, as part of the Edinburgh Festival Fringe in August 2001. An unusual occurrence, even for Edinburgh. The fact that *Of Dogs and Men* has seen the light of day is due to the efforts of

Kirsten Graham, my current editor. Finally, behind every man is a good woman and this is certainly true. I have reached a time of life where I can safely lay the blame for poor recall, confusion of facts and complete omissions, on my age. And for these I take full responsibility and offer my apologies.

By far my biggest vote of thanks must go to all the wonderful dogs I have ever worked with. I never ceased to be amazed by the skill, endurance and sagacity of sheepdogs and collies. Some dogs demonstrate the ability to quite rapidly solve unexpected problems. Hazel, a brown and white Border Collie belonging to one of the Loch Katrine shepherds, had been sent out into the water to recover a fugitive lamb. Approaching the shore, as the water-logged lamb sank lower and swam slower, the bitch was quickly closing in. All Bill McCabe could do was to order Hazel to lie down, and her swimming in ten feet of water! At first Hazel simply slowed, until she was in danger of becoming submerged. But before colliding and overwhelming her quarry, Hazel turned away and began swimming in a flat-eight pattern, thus keeping her station behind the lamb. All ended well. Several years later, in almost identical circumstances, my Bran dog behaved in exactly the same way. A case of great minds thinking alike.

The speed sheepdogs can pick up and assimilate new information can also be surprising. Whilst manning a display stand at a game fair, at Cardross, Central Scotland, two lady dog handlers from the Trossachs Search and Rescue Dog Team took a look at the Gun Dog Scurry. Believing that their dogs, a Border Collie and Hovawart respectively, would not disgrace themselves, just for a bit of fun, the girls entered the competition. At the end of proceedings the Border Collie stood in first place and the German Hovawart was third. With another lady and her Black Labrador taking second spot, the tweed-suited, gun-toting gentry were greatly disgruntled.

Dogs, too, have seemingly embraced the modern age, their attributes utilised in disciplines as diverse as medicine and technology. Roosevelt is a Border Collie in Portland, Maine, who had been born with severely deformed front legs. Just like his namesake, Franklin D. Roosevelt, polio victim and President of the USA (1882–1945), this dog is wheelchair dependent. Used to support his front end, and at a cost of $900, the two-wheeled carriage is certainly not cheap.

To conclude this chapter I must make mention of Ziggy, a Californian red-coated Labrador, with quite remarkable powers. Cork taint in wine is a troublesome and costly problem and not usually traceable until the wine bottle is opened. If present in the cork, an unseen organism will react badly with the contents of the bottle to produce 2, 4, 6–Trichloroanisole. At a low level, this will simply reduce the aromas and flavour of the wine. The worst-case scenario is an expensive wine that smells exactly like a wet, dirty dog. Until Ziggy's nose came into the picture, there had been no way to identify problematic cork. Now there is, at least at one Californian winery.

Sitting with a glass of 1967 Domaine de Chevalier, from Bordeaux, I raise a toast to many years of memories, all my dogs and Luath Press.

Founder

LUATH PRESS WAS FOUNDED in 1981 by a remarkable man named Tom Atkinson. He was born in County Durham in 1922, the son of a police officer based in the mining village of Cockfield. An adventurous youth, at the tender age of 14 Tom ran away from home to enlist with the International Brigade fighting in Spain but was sent home with, no doubt, a flea in his ear. At the outbreak of World War II Tom Atkinson lost no time in enlisting with the Royal Air Force. By 1941, he had volunteered to serve in the RAF Commando Division, frequently working behind enemy lines and laying the groundwork for future gains and advances.

Towards the end of the conflict Atkinson was posted to the Dutch East Indies, to hold the line as the Japanese rapidly withdrew. In no time at all, Atkinson and a close circle of fellow RAF comrades had set up and were operating a Pro-Indonesian group, in full support of Achmad Sukarno. Propaganda leaflets were printed off, to be widely distributed by sympathetic flying crews. Just two days after the unconditional surrender of Japan, Sukarno announced a Unilateral Declaration of Independence. The Dutch were not coming back and Indonesia appeared on the maps of the world.

By 1946 Tom Atkinson was back in the United Kingdom, but still working quite openly for the Bureau of Indonesian Information. Well aware that a significant number of Indonesian nationals, most of whom had laboured on the infamous Burma-Thailand Railway, were still incarcerated as Prisoners of War in Japan, a plan of action was set up. At this point, Tom Atkinson becomes the 20th century version of Sir Percy Blakeney, the Scarlet Pimpernel of his Age. Whilst not actually in Japan, this wily campaigner had several strategies up his sleeve. Questions were even asked in the House of Commons. It was not long before these prisoners were safely repatriated. This was only the start, however, much more intrigue and excitement was to follow.

Newly independent Indonesia, having installed Sukarno as the first President, soon established a swish embassy in Grosvenor Square, with Atkinson and two of his RAF colleagues well and truly ensconced at the heart of affairs. As the situation changed, so did Tom Atkinson's position, becoming President Sukarno's speech writer and spindoctor – now in the guise of a future New Labour's Alistair Campbell. Sukarno's address to the General Assembly of the United Nations, so precisely crafted that Atkinson had written in the natural pauses, stutters and hesitations of the President's normal delivery, was received in New York with a massive standing ovation. But irreconcilable political differences were soon to arise.

The parting of the ways came in 1962, Atkinson finally returning to England with Rene, a former WAAF and now Tom's wife. After ten exotic years putting words into the mouth of a high profile political leader, in 1962 the Atkinsons shook off Indonesia and touched down in a remote spot on the west coast of Scotland and opened a hotel. Glenborrowdale, on the southern shore of Ardnamurchan Peninsula, the most westerly point of mainland Britain, is as beautiful as it is isolated. Overlooking the sheltered waters of Loch Sunart, with breathtaking views of Morven and the Isle of Mull, Glenborrowdale House was soon renovated and open for business. The coffee, rubber and palm oil and Indian Ocean now replaced with blackface sheep, red deer and, hopefully, tourists – and the vagaries of the Atlantic weather.

To paraphrase the words of Neil Armstrong, it was a small step from Ardnamurchan to South-West Wales, and a giant leap from hotelier into farming. Twelve acres at Llanycefn, in the lee of Mynydd Preseli, hills that provided the massive blue stones for Stonehenge, would be the family home throughout the 1970s. With a smallholding of only five hectares, Tom Atkinson used his well-honed talents to augment earnings eked out from Welsh soil. A mainline rail link from Pembrokeshire to London was undoubtedly an important lifeline during this period. The sale of Golden Retriever puppies from the farm also augmented family income. But, after an absence of ten years, the pull of Caledonia could be felt. It was time for the Durham lad and Cockney girl, born within the sounds of Bow Bells, to return to Scotland.

Tom and Rene Atkinson, with daughters Dee and Chanchal, were now to set down new roots in Ayrshire, almost equidistance by road from Glenborrowdale and Llanycefn. Here a new facet would quickly be buffed-up in the life of Tom Atkinson, a lifelong love and appreciation of Robert Burns. Their parallel strands of pen and plough would be drawn together in the foundation of Luath Press.

Luath, spoken as loo-ah in Gaelic, translates as meaning quick, fast or speedy, an appropriate name for any good sheepdog. Historically, Luath was the hunting hound of Cuchullin, one of the great heroes of Erin, and features in many a tale told long ago by Ossian. Our Luath, however, was said to be the favourite sheepdog of Robert Burns, and for very good reason. It was this faithful companion that effected the all-important meeting between the farming poet and Jean Armour, his future, long-suffering wife. The exact circumstances of this introduction are open to quite different interpretation. Either Luath got under Miss Armour's feet during a wedding ceilidh, tumbling the lass into her future husband's arms, or the dog cocked his leg against a pile of Jeanie's freshly washed laundry. Collies and sheepdogs certainly like to lift their leg at any opportunity.

Burns must have really loved that dog. There is a great deal of truth in the statement that if the bond between owner and dog is particularly well developed, they become more and more alike. Luath, exactly like his master, was very fond of the opposite sex, known to sow more than his fair share of wild oats, and leave a good number of offspring around the countryside. Whilst Burns only had to face the wrath of the kirk and irate fathers, a raking dog would have to fight off rivals battling for possession and territory. Blood and fur would frequently fly and, on occasion, fatalities would occur. In the days when dogs roamed more freely, there were many tales told about such dogfights, the victors being highly lauded.

The vanquished would struggle home to lick their wounds or, sometimes, to die. On a harsh night in February 1784, a mortally wounded Luath barely made it back to Mossgiel Farm, only to expire a short time later. If the death of Luath was bad enough, the very next night Burns' father, William Burnes, shook off his mortal coil and also departed this world. To the end of his life, William signed his surname as Burnes. It was in this slough of deep personal sadness that Robert Burns wrote one of his greatest poems, 'The Twa Dogs', the land-working bard at his biting, satirical best. One of the dogs was, of course, called Luath. This was also the name adopted by Tom Atkinson for his own sheepdog, and for his newly-established publishing company, ensconced in the heart of Burns Country.

Although written by Tom, the detailed research involved in the publication of *South West Scotland*, the first title from Luath Press, was a collaborative husband and wife effort. The books were actually put together and bound on the kitchen table, in the family home at Barr. This was just the beginning. Now based in Edinburgh, Luath Press continues to be committed to publishing well written books worth reading.

Learner

I VERY QUICKLY DECIDED that either I was going to spend a great deal of time chasing around after runaway livestock, or I was going to get a dog to do all that chasing for me. At 15 I was in Pembrokeshire, on the threshold of embarking on my chosen career, my first steps to becoming a farmer. Apart from the odd spell of wanting to become an engine driver, soldier or astronaut, being on the land and working with animals had been my overriding ambition. Earliest memories are of being down on the family farm with my paternal great grandfather, Charlie, along with great uncles Willie John and Edgar. Inside the gloomy Gower farmhouse, always lit by a large paraffin lamp standing on the living room table, my great grandmother and great aunt ruled the roost. But it was out in the fresh air that I wanted to be. From an early age I had been fascinated by animals, especially dogs.

In fields grazed by cattle or amongst sheep quietly nibbling the short, tight sward on the cliff tops, overlooking the Brandy Cove, I first began to appreciate the true value of a good sheepdog. Uncle Willie John was full of stories, and tales of their collies, past and present, enthralled me most. There had been Lark, a yellow-coated sheepdog of a kind that, even at that time, had become quite rare. As soon as Lark heard sounds of old fashioned hand-shears being sharpened, the whetstones ringing along the highly tempered blades, without a word he took himself off to begin his work. In no time, about a score of Welsh Mountain ewes carrying full fleeces, startled lambs milling around their legs, would be waiting at the gate to the yard. The clipping was soon underway. By the time that the holding pen had been cleared of ewes, Lark would be back with the next consignment of 20 or so sheep.

Lark was also a good judge of sheep on the hoof. In the days when the local butcher would travel around the countryside, coming two or three times a year to kill a couple of fat animals for the farm's own use, Lark had the opportunity to show off his party piece. As soon as the butcher, mounted on his horse, appeared on the farm track, this sheepdog was moving quietly amongst the ewes and lambs, selecting his target. In anticipation of this day of doom for one of the lambs, and probably a young pig too, the sheep would have been gathered into a paddock adjacent to the buildings. Once Lark picked out his target, the young animal would be quietly manoeuvred and held at the gate, no stress, no fuss, no human. I have been told by several other people that a fatter lamb could not have been found in the flock. A very useful dog.

Ten years along the line, and I was holding in my hands a tiny, almost totally black, Welsh collie puppy. This was Lassie, destined to be my very first sheepdog and the progenitor of the strain which carried me right through my entire career. Rexie, her mother, had whelped in usual fashion, deep in a den excavated below a high-banked, hawthorn hedgerow. The pups were about ten days old before she relocated the litter of seven to the comfort of the barn, eyes already opened. They were soon making themselves at home amongst bales of hay. Knowing both parents, and having a free pick from the litter, it was actually Lassie that made the all important choice. That wee ball of dark fur looked me fully in the eye and used her sorcery on me. I was left with no option. My first duty was to take sole charge of feeding and arrange for her vaccinations, essential for every dog.

Our partnership was almost ended before it began. The surplus puppies from Redberth Farm had, for many years, been bought by a man who turned up one afternoon, behind the wheel of a battered Morris estate car. A nice man and a pleasure to do business with, according to my employer, Mr Jenkins. At the point of departure, and having been told that my pup was still in the barn, I just happened to notice Lassie's forlorn face pressed up against one of the side windows. I reclaimed my little bitch, leaving the dealer heaving and hauling a great many bales, before finally catching the last of his victims. On making a few discreet enquiries through the local Young Farmers' Club, it turned out that the 'nice man' had dealings with several zoos. He never set foot on Redberth Farm again, the pythons needing to be fed from other sources.

At that time I was working on a dairy farm, learning the ropes and appreciating the fact that, if I really put on a sprint, I could just about overtake a milk cow. Young stock were far more evasive. Apart from the usual day to day tasks about the farm, I was given an excellent grounding in drystone dyking. Billy Cobb, an octogenarian, was only too willing to pass his ancient skills on to me. I was also taught to drive. Lassie grew rapidly, her minute white bits expanded and she was becoming a very beautifully marked young bitch. Well, I would say that, wouldn't I? In fact, my grandfather had given me a piece of pertinent advice; if you ever have a dog that you do not like – make sure the dog never finds out! Cows came in and out twice a day for milking, and quite soon the dairy herd and young collie were comfortable with the sight of each other, Lassie keeping close to my heel as we followed the cows to the byre or back to the field. At that stage I was still the gofer until, at about four months old, the pup ran ahead to get behind a particularly slow moving animal loitering at the back of the herd. It was probably a distance of less than ten yards, but it was definitely a start.

In a matter of a few weeks I only had to open the gate to the grazing field and Lassie did the rest, the cows coming out through the gate without any hint of a rebellion. Throughout my working life, the only time I ever encountered problems with livestock was when I was dog-less. It is amazing how they know. Years later, working as a shepherd, there would be occasions when, driving home, I would encounter sheep where there should be no sheep. Making out as if the Land Rover was packed full of dogs, no matter how realistic I could make the cameo drama, even going to open the back door of the vehicle, the brutes would stand their ground. I swear they were laughing their woollen socks off. Drive off to the kennels, load up a couple of dogs and, before we had got anywhere near them, those sheep would already be well on their way back to their own ground. And they say sheep are stupid; not true. They are, however, often infuriating creatures.

Widening my experience, prior to going to agricultural college, Lassie and I were soon working at another farm. The village of Llangennith was on my old stomping ground of Gower, only a few miles from my great grandfather's farm. Although I was still mainly dairying, here there were early potatoes, grain growing, tractor work – and sheep. At first I did not see much of the Welsh Mountain flock, just picking out distant white dots foraging on the slopes of Rhosili Down. A limestone backbone, through which an underlying bed of Old Red Sandstone erupts, runs the length of Gower Peninsula, reaching its highest point at 632ft/193m on our ground. My initial contact with these fairly wild sheep was by going out with someone well versed in their wily ways, Lassie more for show than anything else. Sheep are a quite a different proposition from cows. I soon discovered that six wild, mountain sheep, when faced by a dog, can scatter in at least seven different directions. However, once gathered, a young lad with even an inexperienced pup is far better equipped to deal with sheep than any two men without a dog between them. Any well behaved dog is certainly better than no dog at all.

The day Lassie earned me my spurs is forever etched on my memory. I had been sent out with Elwyn Rees, a neighbouring farmer, to sweep the sheep off the top of Rhosili Down. Below us was a thin line of men, steadily working the sheep forward with their tireless dogs dodging back and forth. The sun shone down and the sea, stretching across the Bristol Channel towards distant Devon, danced with reflected light. All was well with the world. From the hilltop, Elwyn spotted about 30 of our sheep cheekily feeding themselves on the neighbouring farm's grass, an easy enough task for me to take charge of. Lassie set off in style, seeming to know what was expected of her. The sheep had other ideas, immediately stampeding in exactly the opposite direction, their long tails whirling like propellers. In no time at all, sheep and dog had completely disappeared from view. The only thing on the horizon was a solitary, wind-cropped hawthorn. My canny mentor made no comment, just working away with his two Welsh Black and Tan bitches, Fly and Scott. I was crushed and felt about two feet tall.

The flock was beginning to gather together on the lower slopes, having all the appearance of the development of a white cirrus cloud on the hillside. For me, that magnificent summer day had lost all its splendour: it would soon be revealed that I had committed a cardinal sin. I had, at my very first attempt, lost my sheep. Worse than that, I had lost my dog. As Elwyn worked our or, I should rightly say, his sheep through the opening in the stone wall and into the *ffrydd* (the gathering place, translating as mountain field) there was a very heavy weight upon my shoulders. When all seemed to be quite lost, Elwyn called to me to take a look backwards. There, to my astonishment, were the missing sheep and my dog coming hell for leather and, apparently, every one accounted for. That was the moment in which I knew my destiny was to be a shepherd. As fate would have it, I was teamed up with the right dog.

Welsh Black and Tan collies, obviously popular around Llangennith, at the west end of the peninsula, soon caught my attention. Their breeding could be traced back to a dog called Scamp, brought down from the Brecon Beacons not long after World War II. Generally larger and more strongly boned than the Welsh border-type collies, they were even bigger than the Scottish sheepdogs just beginning to make an appearance in the locality. These black and tan marked dogs also worked in a plainer style, not showing the inclination to fix their quarry with a hypnotic stare, often resulting in a stalemate, neither sheep nor dog making any ground. Years elapsed before I fully appreciated the differences between the many distinct strains of sheepdogs and collies found throughout the British Isles.

My employer at that time, Ernie Rees BEM, had a third generation Scamp dog – who answered to Sheber – big, strong and very able. In fact, Sheber had been sent to have his natural talents honed by a Scottish shepherd running sheep over the salt marshes of North Gower, an area famed for the special flavour of its lamb. This could be a treacherous tract for the ignorant or unwary, the tides rapidly sweeping up the Burry Estuary, filling the deep-cut drainage channels before flooding the low-lying land. It takes a really clever sheepdog to skilfully manoeuvre estuary sheep to safety, requiring an innate knowledge of the twice daily tide-table and the ability to take a safe route out of the labyrinth. Every drain is potentially a death-trap. Sheber, I was assured, was just such a dog and the

Scottish shepherd was rather reluctant to send him back when his training was over. I was still very much a novice at this game, but this, I was sure, would provide the future bloodline for me to work with.

During my time at the agricultural college, on the River Usk in Monmouthshire, and having my own dog at hand, I was able to find weekend and evening work alongside the college shepherd, Roger Juke. Hiring out our services to local farms on a contract basis was not only great fun, but I got paid for my efforts. I am pretty sure that, under the guidance of such an experienced man, Lassie benefited as much as I did from my student days at Usk. Although specialising in Dairying and Dairy Science, my interest in sheep was undoubtedly growing stronger. There were opportunities for many hours of dog training as Lassie and I honed our collective skills, mostly in secluded fields at the far end of the college estate. It was a time of considerable learning for both of us. We had encountered only a few of the 62 native breeds of British sheep but had already appreciated that each exhibited quite unique features and characteristics.

Certificates, and a great deal of practical experience, eventually tucked away, our next stop was on the high ground of Radnor Forest. I was still milking cows twice a day, but at the challenging altitude of 1,000ft/305m. Seeing that I came so well equipped, my new employer immediately doubled the number of sheep on Penrochel Farm. These were quite mature ewes of Welsh Mountain and Radnor stock, hardly in the first flush of youth. At this stage in their life, these ewes had proved that, on the exposed mountainsides of Central Wales, they could look after themselves as well as rear their offspring. On the richer pasture found on a dairy farm, these ewes could extend their working lives under easier and more sheltered conditions.

While the females had a pleasant disposition, the same could not be said for the young Suffolk ram. Brought in to sire as many meaty, crossbred lambs as he could manage, not only was he surly but a real heavyweight too. His idea of fun was, on our first encounter, to take advantage of the fact that I was dog-less. The brute wandered surreptitiously to my blind-side, waited until I was busy running the grain from the bulky sack into the feed trough, and charged! Having been unceremoniously flattened, next time I decided to take some protection along with me. I was not at all sure that my experienced collie would be a great deal of use, the Suffolk weighing in about eight times heavier than my bitch. It was amazing. Lassie sized up the situation and, quite literally, kept him off my back. I don't recollect actually saying a word to her, being unaware of any command that could be given in these circumstances. Nevertheless, it certainly saved me any further bruises and embarrassment.

The winter of 1962–63 will be long remembered for the succession of blizzards which swept across the whole of Britain, the opening strike coming on Boxing Day. Landscape features of fence lines and hedgerows disappeared beneath a blanket of deep snow. Our cows were snug in their byre, the sheep, however, were well and truly buried where they lay. It took the best part of a week before we dug ourselves out, at last getting our churns of milk to the main road for collection by the dairy. Not until the weather had settled down did we consider digging out the entombed ewes. Guided by instinct, the sheep had scattered to find shelter as best they could. Now we had to find them. Lassie proved to be absolutely invaluable, sniffing out the hiding places one by one. A great deal of digging ensued. The sheep emerged, hungry but otherwise quite healthy, all except one. Hill sheep are naturally well adapted to survive such harsh conditions, sometimes for weeks on end. Many months later, the still well preserved carcass of the missing sheep was discovered inside the ruins of an old cottage. Not even Lassie could have found her entombed body in there.

Snow still lay in sheltered spots, well into the summer. Plantations of conifers, bulldozed out of the ground en masse, could be regularly heard crashing to earth as the snowdrifts loosened their grip. In the days before tractor cabs, I soon discovered the pleasures of a warm dog wrapped around my kidneys, Lassie squashed behind me in the bucket seat. Morning mists of summer filled the valley below Penrochel and blue skies abounded, as if to make up for the freezing months of winter. After their ordeal our ewes thrived, producing an excellent crop of lambs. The flock mainly foraged on the steep-sided, scrubby valley behind the farm steading. Lassie was well able to bring the sheep in, quite unaided, usually while we had breakfast after the morning milking.

A return to Gower was in the offing, to the same pre-college farm. I was to take charge of the dairy herd, but there would plenty of general farm work as well – and sheep. From Radnor I took a really good grounding in public speaking and a nascent interest in journalism, both thanks to my employer, Cyril Hullin. Although still in thrall to dairy cows, Lassie and I were soon in demand for extra contract work, particularly at busy times. Working with local farmer's son, John Barrow, who became a life-long friend, we were never short of assignments. Needing extra dog power, Lassie produced a couple of litters, the pups sired by Welsh Black and Tan, Sheber. A black and tan bitch pup was kept from each batch, first Bo and then Chris. This was yet another step along the road of sheepdog handling. I had become a breeder.

The Gower Peninsula was designated as the first 'Area of Outstanding Natural Beauty', in 1956. Along with the mosaic farmland, there is moorland, heath land, precipitous cliffs, sand dunes, sandy and pebble beaches, woodlands with freshwater streams and

estuary habitats. College Farm, Llangennith, taking its name from the ancient collegiate church of St Cenydd, had all of these habitats except a pebble beach. The dairy cows were a mixture of Friesian, Ayrshire and Jersey breeds: Lassie brought these milkers in from the fields twice a day. Once I had opened the gate Lassie took complete charge, allowing me to get on with other things. Never hurrying her charges, the cows came steadily homeward in single file, often passing through the village. Traffic could, if they wished, pass the cows, even on a narrow road, and open garden gates would be completely ignored. Most stockmen, usually needing to get on as quickly as possible, would cause the herd to bunch-up, blocking the width of the road and forcing cows to seek refuge in any available garden. This is just one of the cases where a dog is far better than man. The valuable time saved added up to several hours every week.

When it came to working with the Welsh Mountain flock, my boss, Ernie Rees and his son, Edward, each had an excellent working sheepdog. Ernie's Black and Tan Sheber had a penchant for rabbiting. A very soft-mouthed dog, the live rabbit would be carried around the countryside and throughout the village until dog and master met up. By this time Sheber's head would be alive with rabbit fleas. The rabbit, completely unharmed, would more often than not be returned to the wild. Edward's dog was quite different, his Peter being a very fine specimen of a yellow-skinned collie.

Now extremely rare, the last bastion of yellow sheepdogs is limited to isolated pockets on the far west of the British mainland and County Wicklow, in Ireland. Just like their close cousins, the Shetland Sheepdog and Rough Collie, these yellow dogs are double coated. The long, golden guard hairs overlay a thick, dense undercoat, a feature I found being put to good use on the Hebridean island of Lewis – panning for gold.

A crofter, Hamish McDonald, was the owner of such a dog, one, he claimed, to have been far more use to him dead than it had ever been whilst alive. At the end of each summer, the pelt of this yellow dog was carefully secured at the bottom of a nearby burn, skin-side down. Several weeks later, before the autumn deluge threatened to wash it out to sea to feed the salmon, the saturated skin would be lifted out of the water and carried home. Put to dry over an old, slatted clipping stool, in a draughty barn, still skin-side down, the pelt would gradually dry out. Then, placed on a clean, white tablecloth, with the fur-side down, the skin would be vigorously beaten with a short, thick stick called a priest, also used to dispatch freshly caught fish. Peeling back the pelt, a layer of gold dust would be revealed and carefully collected. Hamish assured me that this dog had been pretty useful about the croft but, after his demise, had been literally worth his weight in gold. Note the similarity to the well known Greek legend of the Golden Fleece.

Peter was renowned for several things; being audibly grumpy whenever someone stood near his perpetually sore legs, going a-courting over half of the peninsula, and being smarter than your average dog. He also had a penchant for lifting his hind leg. One notable event began with a meeting of neighbours in the kitchen of the King's Head Hotel, also owned by the Rees family, to plan the next morning gathering of our sheep. All evening Peter had grumbled at anyone who got too close, as he dozed in front of the enormous coal-fired cooker. Next morning there was pandemonium, Peter had slipped out at the first opportunity, and vanished. Plans were in disarray and hurriedly changed. Ernie would take over the milking and I was to take Lassie and go out with now dog-less Edward, who was not in the best of humour. Having already been greatly delayed, there ensued a white-knuckle ride in the Land Rover as we sped to our starting point. As we flashed past the *ffrydd*, Edward jammed on the brakes, neither of us believing what we had just glimpsed. Reversing to the gate, we could see that the small, walled enclosure was crowded with sheep and, just inside the opening to Rhosili Down was Peter, sitting and wagging his tail for all he was worth. His section of the hill had already been gathered. The previous evening he had not only been growling, but listening. A very clever sheepdog, indeed.

The western extremity of Rhosili Down drops steeply to a magnificent three mile sweep of golden sand. To the south of Rhosili Bay is the serpentine Worm's Head, jutting far out into the sea. The high cliffs of Burry Holms, an island marking the northern end of the beach, provides grazing for about two score of our sheep, and is easily accessible for about two hours at low water. Each time we finished a handling at the farm, all the sheep would be turned out, directly down a narrow lane that led back to the bottom of the hill, from where they would soon spread out. The Burry Holms stock would often lie in a group on the face of the Down, patiently waiting for the distant full tide to turn. At this point they would again make tracks, arriving in time to cross dry-shod to their island home. With tides twelve and a half hours apart, those particular Welsh Mountain ewes obviously had perfect knowledge of the tide-table.

Any spare time was taken up by contract work, mostly relief milking duty or handling sheep. On these mostly family run farms, an extra pair of hands was always welcome – especially if they came with a decent dog or two. At harvest time everyone is fully stretched. In those days, winter feed for the animals was predominantly hay. This man and his dog certainly mowed many a meadow, Lassie comfortably alongside me on the wide, wooden bench seat of an old David Brown tractor.

Gower farmers are very neighbourly, and I was occasionally allowed to cover for someone who needed to be somewhere else. One of the more unusual requests came from the young daughter of a farmer at Burry, about four miles distant. Her father and elder brother had gone to London, to attend the annual Smithfield Show. On going to bring their Clun Forest ewes into the covered barn for the cold December night, lambing scheduled to begin in a couple of weeks, most of the sheep were posted missing from their field. By the time I had responded to Heather Austin's telephone call, all daylight had gone.

One by one, Lassie checked out the hedge-lined fields, through which sheep, especially under pressure, can frequently find a way from one side the another. Cluns were gathered from the darkness in dribs and drabs, until only a single sheep was unaccounted for. Explaining the situation to Lassie, as best I could, my bitch took off across the farmhouse garden, dropped down over the wall into the farmyard and disappeared through the gate, turning right onto the road. Following in my Land Rover, I soon picked up Lassie in the headlights, going at a good clip. As I negotiated a right hand bend, I was just in time to see my sheepdog pass and turn the missing ewe back in my direction. The hunt was over, and the last sheep soon joined the others in the comfort and safety of the Dutch Barn. To this day, I have never figured out quite how she did it. The sheep had probably been scattered by a rogue dog and definitely gathered up by a good one.

By this time, Bo was beginning to shape-up nicely, and Chris, a young pup, had arrived on the scene. At this point, Elwyn Rees, whose advice I always valued, put me in an absolute quandary. I was told that I ought to sell Lassie. Although I had not been short of offers, I had never even contemplated that as a possibility. My blood ran cold with the thought of it. However, Elwyn assured me that unless I parted with my constant companion who had served me so well, and to whom I owed so much, the younger dogs would not reach their full potential. Lassie, as long as I kept her, would always be expected to bear the brunt of the work. Wise words, indeed. Lassie was sold to Colin Gordon, a local dairy farmer, but one who was beginning to develop an interest in sheepdogs and sheepdog trials. The price was fair, but my heart was heavy, cheered only by the fact she had gone to a really good new handler.

The advice that I had been given proved to be true enough. Bo soon took up the challenge and, in no time at all, was doing everything her mother could do, and a little bit more. Sturdier than Lassie, and with vibrant tan markings on her face and legs, I found myself with an even better dog. Chris was coming on a-pace, too. With the prospect of a full order book, I turned to full time contracting and certainly now had need of two good sheepdogs. I quickly appreciated that from their father, Sheber, the Welsh Black and Tan bloodline had greatly improved stamina levels, essential when working hill ground, moorland and the two and a half thousand acres (1,000 ha) of tidal marshes. Alongside John Barrow, from Tankey Lake Farm, the summer of 1966 was going by in endless sunny days. Sheep were gathered and sheared in their hundreds, lambs marked and dipped. Then, one afternoon, at a farm at

OF DOGS AND MEN

Llanrhidian, the last ewe was divested of her wool and all the pens were standing empty. There would be a lull for a week or two, until the hay making and potato picking got underway, time for a well earned holiday.

My plan was to head north, maybe as far as Scotland, to investigate the possibility of extending the next shearing season by working our way up the map. I had never been north of the Border. Before I could set off, there were one or two loose ends to be tied up. The most important of these, I'm afraid, involved Lassie, who had recently become quite unwell. Colin Gordon agreed that I should take her back and see what could be done. In short, not a lot. Failing to respond to treatment, there was only one course of action left. It was up to me to carry it through, as much for myself as for Lassie. To the very end, Lassie made things easier for me, calmly looking away from me as I pulled the trigger. As I stood and listened to the silence, the world seemed to stand still. I realised that I had just completed my first full cycle in being a dog handler. Lassie was laid to slumber in the warm Gower soil, facing west into the sunset and the Pembrokeshire land of her birth.

Leaving Gower for just a short break, Bo and Chris in the back of my new A35 van, we passed Stembridge Farm, Lassie's last home, little realising that I would be gone for a while longer than expected. I would be returning to Gower, and certainly coming back to Stembridge Farm.

Shepherd

'SHEPHERD', PROCLAIMED THE JOB description on the cover of my brand new Clydesdale and North of Scotland Bank passbook, inscribed in the manager's copperplate handwriting. I was suddenly a fully-fledged member of the second-oldest profession in the world. This tiny bank served the small village of Hatton, Aberdeenshire – a cluster of houses, a police station and a biscuit factory. There was no longer a station, but the Station Hotel next to the redundant bridge was still very much open for business. It was in the bar of this hotel that my life took a complete change of direction. A local farmer, enjoying a well-earned evening pint, asked about my two collies, curled up quietly at my feet. On hearing that they were indeed working dogs and not just pets, I was invited take a meal at his place, and maybe show off the ability of my dogs. A paddock in front of the farmhouse held about a score of North Country Cheviot tups. These are males of the species kept for breeding, and not the easiest of animals to work with. Four gates were tied together to serve as a pen. Having been asked to shed off the half a dozen youngest tups, just coming to their first shearing, while Chris kept control of the rest, Bo soon had her sheep in the pen. Could we do the reverse, putting the four oldest, and most obdurate, tups into the pen? Yes, of course. There was much stamping of feet and a bit of whistling down the nose, but Bo was taking no nonsense and in they eventually went. Finally, a succession of individual tups were pointed out and, one by one, brought to hand. After such a display, I felt that supper had been properly earned.

This was my introduction to Scottish hospitality. Not only was I scrumptiously fed and watered, my host had arranged for me to meet a farmer friend of his, one in need of a shepherd. This is how I came to be surveying my new domain, Berrylea Farm, high on the Moss of Cruden and looking east to a distant panorama of the North Sea. The spire of St James, standing above Cruden Bay, was clear to see, and would become quite significant. No strong drink could be served on the Sabbath – except to bona fide travellers on a journey of at least three miles. A Sunday morning sojourn to the kirk, and then home via the Station Hotel, was well within the letter of this peculiar law. Along with a traditional, granite-built farmhouse came a flock of North County Cheviot ewes and a beef herd of Blue-Grey suckler cows. Shepherd and dogs found themselves facing completely new and exciting challenges.

Moss, mainly of the sphagnum variety, slowly decomposes to peat at the rate of one millimetre a year. Berrylea stood on a few millennia's worth of this mouldered vegetation and, although drainage had been carried out, the ground was still waterlogged. A tractor had at one time been totally submerged in the bog, and never recovered. Mainly a grass farm for grazing livestock, a small acreage of cereal was grown for winter feed. We needed a really good frost in the ground before heavy machinery could finish off the last of the harvest. The adjoining Moreseat Farm was also owned by my new employer, and with better soil, it was an arable unit growing potatoes, cereal and grass for silage. One of the perks of my new job was to be provided with a house-cow, also a Blue-Grey, bred from a white Shorthorn bull and black Aberdeen Angus dam. No milking machine here, this girl expected to be milked by hand. With a constant round of dosing against internal parasites, dipping to remove external bloodsuckers and interminable feet-trimming, Bo and Chris were getting plenty of sheep work. And after extricating the third ewe from a deep drainage ditch, I was beginning to realise just how keen sheep are to die. If dying was an Olympic event, sheep would have been going home with gold medals since the days of Ancient Greece.

The communities of North-East Scotland, an area known as Buchan, are exceptionally hospitable, and gossip, now called net-working, was rife and widespread. This is how I came to hear of an interesting vacancy at Aberdeen University Farm: a Shepherd/Instructor was required. Before long I was moving to Tillycorthie Farm, on the outskirts of Udny Station, 12 miles north of Aberdeen. Not only did I have to manage a very intensive sheep regime, I was responsible for instructing BSc (Agriculture) students in the practical aspects of sheep husbandry. There were individual flocks of pure North Country Cheviot and Dorset Horn ewes, along with cross-bred Scottish Halfbred and Greyface units. A number of pure-bred sheep would be put to tups of their own kind, to breed replacement stock. Everything else was crossed with either Dorset Down or Suffolk tups, their lambs all destined for the butcher. Tillycorthie also had a good little export trade, sending Dorset Horn tups to the Shetland Isles. Now I was really busy and certainly did not need to count sheep at night before falling asleep.

Then there were the Shetland sheep, just a few, which initially caused me and my two dogs more aggravation than all the others put together. Shetlands are small, cunning, and have the ability to stray from field to field, apparently at will. The very first time Bo and Chris filled up the sheep pens for me, the ringleader of the renegades jumped onto the backs of larger sheep and skipped out over the side. Of course, the rest of the Shetlanders followed suit. However, I had a cunning plan. Letting the sheep out of the fank and bringing the escapees back to join them, I only used Chris to return them all to the holding pen. Bo was asked to lie down exactly where the first sheep had landed, ready for an instant repeat performance. On command, Bo caught hold and held fast to the troublemaker. The rest of the bunch were stopped in their tracks. I lifted the Shetland ewe back into the pen – and she never jumped out again. Shetland sheep are one of our more primitive breeds, naturally quite wild, but keep them well-dogged and they will behave beautifully. That was just the beginning of a long love affair with the Shetland breed.

A considerable amount of research was being conducted at Tillycorthie. I became directly concerned with the study of different grazing schemes and feeding programmes for sheep, and all the attendant paperwork. There was a separate study of mineral metabolism in cattle and an involvement in pioneering heart transplant surgery, involving dogs. The actual location of the kennels for these post-operative animals was a well-guarded secret. In South Africa, Christian Barnard was yet to conduct his first human heart transplant. Dealing with undergraduates was fairly straightforward.

Most of them were keen to get to grips with basic tasks, from fencing off paddocks for grazing, to the end product – selecting lambs for slaughter. Every single student, though, was fascinated by the integral role of the working collie. They could see that handling sheep would be practically impossible without them, and no therapist better than a sheepdog licking your face.

Moving sheep around the large university estate involved a great deal of road work. Although officially listed as a minor road, the B999 carried a lot of traffic – and mostly at speed. I would walk in front of the flock to confront oncoming vehicles, Bo and Chris steadily working the sheep behind me. One thing was for sure, both of my sheepdogs were well-covered by insurance; buying a working replacement would have been expensive. The main problem was the sheer impatience shown by a minority of motorists. We must have travelled many miles over tarmac, fortunately without any degree of mishap, although it was rather wearing on the dogs' pads.

At the local Whitecairns Sheepdog Trials, I discovered just what a lonely place it can be, standing out at the starting post of your very first trial. The appearance of the university shepherd to start his run seemed to instantly empty the beer tent, and that really didn't help matters. In all honesty, I cannot remember anything about our run, apart from shaking uncontrollably. Bo, however, must have performed pretty well in spite of my inertia, carrying off the trophy for the best novice, a dog never previously placed at an open trial. A question now frequently cropping up was people wanting to know if either of my dogs were registered with the International Sheep Dog Society (ISDS). In short, no, but the little bitch pup at home was. Andrew Sutherland, my predecessor, had sold me my first Scottish Border Collie, called Sian, complete with the prerequisite certificate. Andrew and his wife Bella were originally from Shetland, which accounted for the dissolute Shetland sheep at Tillycorthie. They were, however, excellent sheep for training dogs on.

As he had relocated to take charge of sheep at Craibstone, the North of Scotland College farm, Andrew was not too far away. Taking me under his wing from the start, I was given a great deal of guidance in both sheep and sheepdog handling, and a lot of

Bella's wonderful home baking. I found Sian to be seriously lacking the power I look for in dogs, but still useful to have at hand in case of a misadventure to either Bo or Chris. It was through owning Sian that I became a life member of the ISDS, apparently I had to be properly registered too. Andrew, with his wide circle of contacts, eventually pointed me in the direction of John Campbell, at Ardgay in Sutherland. The dog in which I was particularly interested was called Cap, soon to win a place in the national team. Cap was a strong, take-no-prisoners, type of collie – and he was handsomely marked black and tan. Campbell's Cap sired a litter of pups from Bo and, not long after, was the father of Thane, a spirited bundle of fluff who arrived off the north train at Aberdeen Station. Thane would become my first stud dog, bringing with him some of the very top bloodlines.

The intensively managed ewes at Tillycorthie, kept several sheep to an acre, were expected to rear an average of two and a half lambs each. This was a marked change from the extensively kept hill sheep, which had several acres each, where if every ewe had one lamb, and raised that lamb, it would be an acceptable return. Towards the end of February, as the lambing season approached, the large flock would be divided into smaller groups, according to due date. Each afternoon the batch scheduled for imminent delivery, anytime over the next fortnight, were brought into a floodlit lambing paddock. As ewes lambed, mother and offspring would be put under cover for the night, into cosy, well-bedded, individual pens. Once underway, lambing was a round-the-clock performance, continuing for the next eight weeks. Jimmy Taylor, the farm manager, shared duties with me, especially over the long night shifts. He was the best man I ever saw amongst sheep who never had need of a dog.

Jimmy must have been born with extra special powers, as he could also dowse for water. However, I certainly was in need of a good lambing dog, one with the ability to work amongst sheep without spooking them. To have a dog that could face right up to a ewe, standing its ground, until the shepherd can get hands on the sheep, is often a lifesaver. A stuck lamb, half in and half out, will soon come to grief if the ewe has to be chased any distance before assistance can be given. Sheep being sheep, there will be lulls when nothing happens at all. Then all hell will break loose with ewes lambing all around, usually as the weather takes a turn for the worse. On a March night, during the graveyard watch, it snowed heavily. When things settled down, there was no sign of Bo, who had been doing duty with me. As I whistled, she emerged from under a deep snowdrift, a snug enough retreat on such a wild night. The lights switched off, I could go home for a few hours' snooze in the armchair, Jimmy would be coming along in a while, to hold the fort until the cold light of dawn.

The students who studied agriculture at Aberdeen came from far and wide, with a good sprinkling of overseas scholars. It fell only to the farm manager and shepherd to take charge of any instruction in the practical side of their course work. There was never a shortage of things to teach. Sheep kept so intensively must be dosed and dipped and have their feet regularly trimmed, followed by a walk through a copper sulphate or formalin footbath. Keeping crippling foot rot at bay was an endless task. The overall health of any flock is fundamental in getting the maximum return from the feed consumed. At the end of the day, income from wool, meat, and lambs sold on for breeding, should leave some margin over the total outlay. I also spent some time on the feeding and management of sheepdogs, again pointing out that regular worming, flea control and keeping vaccinations up to date are essential. There were tips on dog handling too. The motto of the International Sheep Dog Society states that there is no good shepherd without good dogs, an old French proverb.

Students at Tillycorthie kept me on my toes, often challenging, always rewarding. Looking back, it is surprising just how often we would find ourselves working in the vicinity of the local inn at lunch time. Purely coincidental. The life of a student seemed to be a lot of fun, as well as requiring a degree of application, and I was becoming of a mind to join their ranks. Four years as a full-time student would be a complete change of lifestyle and, although I reduced the number of dogs I had on hand, dogs would still be needed. Bo had produced a fine litter of nicely marked pups, all showing the black and tan pattern of both parents. I kept one for myself, Arian, the liveliest little bitch pup, the other seven being sold off after weaning. Even lacking paperwork, puppies were sent from Somerset to Shetland, and from Lincoln to the Hebrides. I also sold Sian, complete with her registration certificate and, hardest of all, parted with Chris.

George Christie from Finzean (pronounced fing-an) came to buy one of the puppies, needing a dog with the potential to work suckler cows. During discussion George told me that he already had a collie and corgi at home, both of them too frightened of the cattle to be of any use. A puppy, I told him, would pick up the same traits from his other dogs, but I could sell him a fully trained bitch. Chris was well used to dealing with hill cows, from her Gower days and at Berrylea. In her new home, Chris immediately got off to a good start. Hardly through the door, a deep-throated growl broke up a quarrel between young son and daughter as to who was going to feed Chris her next biscuit. I don't know what the children made of it but the parents fully approved of the intervention.

George worked Boghead Farm with his father but lived at Mid-clune, a croft on the hillside overlooking Finzean. It was here that problems kept arising. No sooner had George driven off in the morning, his hill cows would wander down with one thing in mind. Probing the hedge-line, separating hungry mouths from growing crops, they would soon find a weak spot and break through. Mary, George's wife, seemed to spend a great deal of her time chasing out cows from fields, and filling in the trampled breaches as best she could. Chris, on her first morning, was soon in action – the beasts were in the turnips. The cows, quite used to getting the better of any dog, were rapidly disabused by Chris and hunted out to the hillside. The hole was patched up, the victors returning to the house, Mary well pleased with the first encounter of the day. A few hours elapsed before the cows and calves were once again feeding themselves on turnips. Mary struggled into her Wellington boots and, stout stick in hand, looked around for Chris. Chris was nowhere to be seen. The old team of collie and corgi were pressed back into service and Mary set off once more to do battle. The field, however, was empty, apart from rows of neeps, not a cow or calf in sight. Chris had already chased the raiders out and harassed them halfway up the hillside before Mary called her off. And that was that, the Midclune cows never came through a hedge or over a fence again.

It was not long before George's father turned up at my door quite anxious to buy a pup, one that would turn out like Chris. There were no other dogs at Boghead, so off went a dog pup, soon answering to Sharp. In fact, every dog that the old father ever owned had been called Sharp. Along with the puppy, I had provided a written list of the commands which the young dog would need to learn, along with a few training hints. I was soon told, by a few disgruntled folk, that Sunday morning was dog-training time at Boghead. Whilst the good people of Finzean were looking forward to a bit longer in bed on the Sabbath, cries of, 'Bye to me, Sharp' and 'Away to me, Sharp', interspersed with yells of, 'Lie down, Sharp', shattered the peace of that scattered community. The tuition was rewarded when, one dark and wild winter's night, a motorist knocked at the farmhouse door to report that there were cattle wandering all over the road. Pulling on boots and a full set of waterproofs, lighting an old paraffin lamp, and finding a good stick, the farmer looked for his dog. Sharp, however, was not there. Stumbling out into the storm, the Farmer was amazed to find his beasts already rounded up and milling about in the farmyard. Sharp had slipped out when his master had answered the door, and got on with his job. Mr Christie remarked that he had need of a dog like Sharp sixty years earlier. I took that as a compliment.

In the meantime, Chris at Midclune was not to be outdone by her nephew. One Saturday, while the family were away, their old sow escaped from her sty. The pig, too, had been driven off to the top of the hill, well out of harm's way. Had the sow made her way into the barn there would have been utter chaos, bags of feed ripped open, things turned upside down, a lot of damage in a very short time. Chris had always acted as my number two dog; at Finzean she had quickly developed to reach her full potential. Echoes of the advice Elwyn Rees had once given me.

I had settled into a caravan sited on Mid Ardoe Farm, Banchory Devenick, on the south side of the River Dee, in exchange for relief milking duties. It was conveniently situated for getting to and from my lectures. Neighbouring dairy farmers were also keen on using my services, so Bo and Arian were frequently found working with herds of Friesian cows. But even well-handled dairy cows can get up to mischief, especially if no dog is around. One morning, at the crack of dawn, Ewan Mitchell was banging urgently at my door. About half an hour before, Ewan had opened the gate to the cows' field, calling them in for milking. He had seen the first few ambling towards the byre and had gone into the dairy to assemble the milking machines. At this point his cows went walkabout, quietly passing the byre door and disappearing down the road. Taking Bo with me, we jumped into Ewan's car and followed the tell-tale trail of steaming cow-pats. The renegades were spotted, crowded into the garden of a far off riverside mansion. From a safe distance, Bo was sent off to extricate our herd from what had been manicured lawns and well-tended flower beds. Ewan and I made ourselves scarce. Twenty minutes later the cows began to stroll into their stall, not the least bit perturbed by their unscheduled adventure and with no drop in milk yield. Several of our dairying neighbours, relatively closer to the scene of devastation, received telephone calls from that irate householder. We were just far enough removed to escape unscathed!

The 1971 Scottish National Sheepdog Trials were held at Hazelhead Park, Aberdeen, and I was serving on the organising committee. My main role was to borrow, and arrange the transport of, 300 Scottish Blackface hoggs – last year's ewe lambs and future breeding stock – for each of the three days. That involved several weeks of touring around the countryside with Bo and Arian looking at possible candidates, and making sure they were sound in wind and limb. I paid special attention to their feet; competitors at this level would not thank you for a lame sheep in their cluster of five. I found six sheep farmers each willing to lend around 150 young hoggs. Recently sheared for the first time and all coming off hill ground, they were pretty evenly matched. These sheep, I hoped, would ensure Scotland selected the strongest possible team to compete at international level.

A local livestock haulage firm provided a two-deck lorry, known in those parts as a float, along with a driver experienced in the ways of sheep. There was a straightforward system in place. A load of hoggs would come to Hazelhead each evening, allowing the sheep to settle overnight and be fresh for the next day. Subsequent batches would arrive on site during the day and have sufficient time to relax before being called into action. Once used, the sheep would be herded onto the waiting float for a homeward journey. Simple enough and, until the evening before the final day, it worked like a charm. As that long day faded to a short, summer night, where I expected to find about seven score of blackfaced hoggs peacefully grazing, I was faced by both an empty field and an even emptier feeling in the pit of my stomach. Before me flashed a vision of sheep heading to the bright lights of Aberdeen city centre – a Friday night out. Thane's breeder, John Campbell, from Ardgay, had parked his caravan in an adjacent field for the duration of the trials and, feeling somewhat like Little Bo Peep, I got him out of bed. The terrible truth was soon revealed. Thinking he was being helpful, John had herded the fresh hoggs onto a lorry, and watched the tail-lights disappear into the gloaming. The oft quoted Robert Burns statement, about the well-laid plans of mice and men, certainly came to my mind.

For the next hour or so the telephone wires around Aberdeen must have been red-hot. Unable to intercept the missing animals before they had been turned back out onto their hill, I desperately needed an alternative plan. The contractor arranged for hoggs to be on the field at least a couple of hours before the first run of that all-important last day. Halfway through proceedings, I loaded up enough used sheep and sent them off. An hour or so later the same float, with the same sheep, returned. By running some of those a second time, I had just enough hoggs to see out the day. After three days in their hot seats, the two judges announced their verdicts. Led by the new Scottish Champion, Thomson McKnight, a team of 15 good men and their dogs, a reserve member and two handlers to run a pair of dogs in the brace competition, would proudly represent their country in Cardiff. The International Sheepdog Championship is widely recognised as the pinnacle of achievement. Hosted that year by Wales, John Murray out-manoeuvred the flighty Welsh Mountain sheep, and with his dog, Glen, took the Supreme International Championship back to Scotland. Thomson McKnight proudly returned from Cardiff with the Team Trophy, Scotland having seen off the best that England, Wales and Ireland had to offer.

None of this could have been accomplished without many sheepdogs, and the people assisting them. The flock masters and shepherds prepared to take sheep off their hills, and then see them safely loaded onto the transport. Fellow committee members took responsibility for correctly presenting each packet of sheep to exactly the right place for the competitors, and swiftly taking them off the course at the end of every run. With 50 singles and a few doubles to get through every day, time was of the essence. Bo, Arian and Thane had got through their fair share of work, energy levels never flagging. A great deal of this stamina is down to the Black and Tan breeding, and partly due to their food. For some time I had moved away from feeding my dogs on oatmeal, provided as part of a shepherd's pay, and had been hand-mixing my own fully balanced ration. This recipe had been formulated for me by nutrition experts at Aberdeen University. From a small beginning, this little project had soon developed into a syndicate with half a dozen or so members. Along with the full report of trial proceedings at Hazelhead Park, published in the *Scottish Farmer*, there was an article about my revolutionary dog feed, written by Matt Mundell. Today such complete dog feeds are commonplace.

I was seldom to be seen without my sheepdogs somewhere around. They were always quite content to remain in the motor if they had to, but never on any of the seats. In decent weather a well shaded place out of doors would suit even better, and they were always more than welcome on field excursions. My dogs could be useful too. On one very cold afternoon, during a university botany excursion on the Sands of Forvie, an east wind sliced in from the North Sea, and not even the highest dunes could afford shelter from the snell blast. The professor sensibly decided on an early retreat but no amount of shouting and arm waving could catch the attention of a second group of students, working a little way off with Dr Jarvis. Bo was despatched to round them all up and bring them back to the main party. Then it was off to the pub at Collieston – to discuss the fruits of our endeavours, of course.

On another occasion a lecturer, who had taken his family away overnight, asked me to keep an eye on his empty house. Driving over after dark, I was surprised to find the empty house full of youngsters, seemingly intent on holding an all-night party. As I watched, a few more youths arrived, rang the bell, and were admitted. I did, however, have a plan. Leaving Arian and Thane to block off any escape via the back door, and with Bo at my side, I too rang the doorbell. While I was confronting some of the startled reprobates, Bo moved away and looked down the far side of the house: the ringleaders were leaving through a window. That had been the method of entry. Calling on them to come back, I was told what I could do with myself! Telling them I would send a dog, I was told what I could do with my dog! But back they did come, stumbling out of the night with a big, Black and Tan sheepdog hard at their heels. Late comers who rang for admittance, finding Bo at their back, were invited in to join the rest of the gathering. Once names and addresses had been recorded, the miscreants were sent out into the night, with the reminder that Bo and Arian would be guarding the premises until the owners returned.

Throughout the summer months, Bo picked up a few minor prizes at sheepdog trials around Aberdeenshire, and occasionally took home a trophy for the mantelpiece. I received a lot of encouragement from established dog handlers, not least from Andrew Sutherland at Craibstone and Sandy Alexander, Lady Grant's shepherd, based at Monymusk. It was through the auspices of Sandy Alexander that I became involved in my first sheepdog demonstration, at Fettercairn, in Angus. On the Howe of Mearns, Fettercairn is noted for a distillery, founded in 1824 and only the second ever to be officially licensed. For the first hundred years this distillery was in the hands of the Gladstone family, future prime minister William Gladstone entering Parliament in 1832, as a Tory member. Not surprising, then, that the distillery remains a major sponsor of the Fettercairn Conservative Association annual fête. Sandy and I turned up on a blisteringly hot day, and took the precaution of running excess steam out of the lively blackfaced sheep provided for the occasion. Sandy's Queen and my Bo ran them around in a nearby field, until they became a touch more biddable. In front of Lord Hailsham, Queen worked her sheep well for Sandy, while I gave a commentary over the public address system. Later in the afternoon, thankfully cooler, the roles were reversed as I put Bo through her paces. It must have gone reasonably well because David Myles, who owned the exhibition sheep, himself a future Member of Parliament, placed an order for a pup from Bo's next litter. At Fettercairn I learned that at a sheepdog trial you have to be in the prize list to take home money, at a demonstration you will always get paid.

A change of address, to a council smallholding on the northern edge of Aberdeen, brought about a completely unexpected direction in my life with sheepdogs – guide dogs for the blind. With a firm demand for puppies, Bo and Arian duly produced litters sired by Thane, born within days of each other. One male pup immediately stood out as being a little bit special. Not having the time or facilities to bring Cap on myself, and reluctant to send him on to where his obvious potential may not be fully developed, it was suggested that I contacted the Royal National Institute for the Blind. The Princess Alexandria Centre at Forfar accepted Cap, on the condition that I undertook to puppy-walk him. Steered by Steve Wright, the head trainer, and assisted by a few fellow students, Cap made great progress. By ten months old he could tell the difference between a letter with or without a postage stamp, either leading the way to the nearest postbox or to the post office in order to buy a stamp. Allowed into shops and supermarkets, Cap's ability to remember layout and product placement was uncanny. Puppy-walking led on to more formal training, necessitating me working blind with Cap in harness. I was surprised how quickly I adapted to 'seeing' through my left arm. Little old ladies would offer to help me cross the road. The ability of that sheepdog to listen to and analyse overheard conversations was brought home the day he caught a bus in the city centre without me. While I was worrying about Cap, he had calmly taken himself off the bus at the university sports ground, where I was due to meet friends for lunch. And there he waited until I belatedly turned up, my colleagues wondering how Cap had arrived before there was any sign of me. Not long after, Forfar took charge of his final training and began the search for Cap's new owner. Cap successfully teamed up with a 26-year-old blind/deaf lady, and went to continue his work at Peterlee, in County Durham.

Through my particular interest in mineral and vitamin metabolism, I fell into the lap of a Cheshire-based company, planning on expanding their business into Scotland. Not only did I have a firm grounding in their product lines but, especially through my dogs, I had developed a wide network of contacts. My intimate knowledge of the highways and byways across the North-East corner of Scotland was also an advantage. Always one or more dogs would be travelling with me, curled up in the footwell of the front passenger seat. We were frequently asked to give a helping hand at a farm, sometimes just for a few hours, occasionally a whole day. My dogs thoroughly delighted in these opportunities to work with sheep or cattle. For some reason my head office in the Wirral was not nearly so enamoured. Did I want to wear a suit and drive a car most of my days, or become a shepherd on the Southern Upland hills, the birth place of the Border Collie?

My old Land Rover pulled into Cramallt Farm, snug in Megget Valley, beneath Dollar Law (2682ft/817m) and Broad Law (2756ft/840m). Five dogs spilled from the back of the motor, while Maggi, James and Victoria eased out of the front seat and looked around at our new family home. This was a joint herding, three flocks of Scottish Blackface sheep to share between Maggi and myself, and a sure-footed Welsh Garron horse to help us cover the ground. Hill sheep in the Borders are precisely managed, each hirsel being discrete, and then subdivided into hefts by natural boundaries. Hefted ewes are encouraged to stay within their strictly defined limits, and twice a day herding was essential to maintain this regime, out in the early morning to move sheep off the high ground, and again in the evening to hunt them back up. To cope with this extra work load, I had bought Mona and Max, Border Collie mother and son, from Sandy Alexander and, along with Bo, they would be my team to cover East Cramallt and West Cramallt hirsels. Maggi would work with Thane and bring on the young, home-bred Gail as she shepherded adjacent Meggat Knowes. On that hill they were walking in the footsteps of the greatest of all sheepdog handlers, JM Wilson, winner of nine Supreme International Championships. But for World War II, there would surely have been several more.

These Southern Upland hills are Silurian deposits of sedimentary sandstone, formed about 400 million years ago, and heaved up from the sea bed. Wild mountain thyme grows in abundance to be aromatically crushed underfoot and, if you reached the highest ground early enough to be there before the birds, elusive cloud berries could be picked and eaten. These spacious, gently rounded summits are the highest points in the Borders. A shepherd and his dogs could easily find a circuit of two miles without the least change in altitude, and it is ground on which sheep are easily seen.

The hirsels on either side and across the Megget Water belonged to the same estate, so there was plenty of extra help on hand for gathering sheep. Coming in with the Meggat Knowes hirsel for the lamb marking, the farm manager spotted a single ewe and lamb that had been left behind, high up and quite a long way back. With everything in front of us well under control, I sent Mona away on a long outrun – and promptly forgot about her. We had a fair distance to drive the ewes and young lambs, off the hill and down the road to the fank at Cramallt. After breakfast it was all hands to the pumps, lambs were shed off and their ears marked to identify the hirsel. Tails were also docked and male lambs castrated. All sheep not mothering lambs would be sheared and the wool packed away. About halfway through the morning, Jock Anderson, the manager, spotted a ewe with a very young lamb standing in the road outside the fank. And there too was Mona, having quietly worked the pair home unaided, a distance of over two miles. She collected a bagful of brownie points that morning.

Even in those days there were a few hirsels not actively herded, a contract shepherd being brought in to cover for the lambing period. Ewes will soon lose the hefting habit and freely stray off their proper beat. One young lambing shepherd, Andy, came across exactly that situation. On his first morning he spotted a small cut of ewes, looking suspiciously on the wrong side of a march burn. Andy whistled. The sheep casually lifted their heads and stood their ground, chewing contentedly on the grass in their mouths. A dog was fired out in their direction. The ewes idly lifted their tails, had a piss, then a shit, and only began to amble away as the dog got near. Only this was a particularly powerful dog, who took great delight in hammering the trespassers well over the water and onto their proper heft. Some weeks later, on his very last round, Andy discovered a significantly smaller number of the same sheep again off their ground. He only needed to whistle. The ewes immediately took flight, spitting out the stolen grass and pissing and shitting as they high-tailed it across the burn to safety. No dogging was required. Without a full-time shepherd they would soon have reverted to their wandering ways.

Jean, the Cramallt horse, was not ridden out every day, but one thing I quickly appreciated was, if you are herding on horseback, you need to take an extra dog. You will be covering more ground and travelling that much faster. Jean was particularly useful on early-morning gathering days. James and Victoria, still quite small, could comfortably fit into the saddle and come to the hill with us. Enjoying the experience, the children made themselves useful at the buchts, a system of drystone walls and pens where each heft would be sorted out and handled. The children would ride home in time to take off the tack, turn Jean out into a paddock, and catch the school bus to Yarrow. This was shepherding as I had never known it, a learning curve for man, dogs and small children. My strangest new skill was the ability to sew a small, woollen chastity blanket over the tail and across the back-end of every home-wintered hogg; lambing at too early an age was not desirable. Washing these 'breeks' after they had been worn for quite a while was a very, very unpleasant task!

As the children grew, even having a handy horse, the logistics became ever more difficult to handle. The joint herding in the Borders had been a very worthwhile experience, but our time on the Wemyss and March Estates was coming to an end. On a point of shepherding etiquette, I took away with me the understanding that no man should ever interfere with another shepherd's endeavour, no matter how severe the difficulties he was facing, unless invited to do so. This ancient convention would link us to a history of our next stamping ground, the rugged Perthshire landscape known as the Trossachs. This was MacGregor territory.

The window fitted into one of the gun-ports, in the back wall of our new abode displayed the motto 'E'en do and spare not', meaning, don't talk about it, do it! Alexander I, disarmed and floored by a wild boar he was hunting, invited any one of his loyal subjects to come to his assistance. Malcolm MacGregor sprang

into action and uprooted an oak sapling, holding the irate creature at bay long enough for the king to regain his feet, his spear and some of his dignity. This is the branch of Clan Gregor which settled in Glengyle some 200 years later, bringing with them the royal proclamation as their motto, and the oak tree rather than a pine displayed on their version of clan crest. Rob Roy MacGregor was born at Glengyle in December 1660. On the north-west corner of Loch Katrine, my new ground topped-out at Meall Mór (2450ft/ 747m) and covered four square miles of mountain, the domain of eagle, raven and ptarmigan.

My Glengyle hirsel comprised 750 Scottish Blackface breeding ewes, plus 220 hoggs, although, because of the harsher environ-ment, these young sheep were wintered away from home. There were 24 hardy Highland-cross suckler cows. Twice-a-day herding was not feasible on this terrain, but when on the hill I still kept to the guiding principle of making for the highest ground in the morning. It had been a long time, and a great many miles travelled, since I pocketed that bankbook in Hatton, telling the world I was a shepherd. Guided by many wiser heads, human and canine, my long apprenticeship had come to fruition. Not only was I a hill shepherd, I had the dogs to prove it. Bo was still very much my top dog, supported by Arian's daughter, Gail, and two of Gail's offspring, Boot and Dust. This had taken me to the fourth and fifth generation of my own sheepdog breeding. Also from the same line, Maggi Du (pronounced dee and meaning black), a puppy off Chris, had arrived from Finzean to join my team. Sandy Alexander's Mona and Max completed the kennel, Max now doubling as my stud dog and the father of both Boot and Dust.

On the first day of December, 16 tups, including a few of the hardier Swaledale breed, would be put to the hill, opening a new calendar year for the shepherd. Boot excelled at holding the bulk of very keen tups together on the open hillside, while a lucky pair would be shed off here and there and driven away to start their duties. Commencing this task on the Low End of Glengyle, over the next few hours we would work our way towards the farthest point north, dropping off tups along the way. Even if I had been away for quite a while, depending on how far I needed to go with my charges, Boot would keep his sheep well contained, until all had been safely dispersed. A daily round during the shortest days of the year was essential, making sure that the tups were doing what tups should be doing. That is where a lambing percentage actually begins. Fresh tups are turned out at 17 days and the worn-out boys begin to come home. Hoggs grow into gimmers and, at just under two years old, encountering tups for the first time, are notoriously shy breeders. Gathering one section of my hill at a time, the ewes were shed off to stay out and the tups and gimmers were brought home, the young sheep to be closely confined with the tups for a while longer. Even so, come May, there would be more gimmers without lambs at foot than the rest of the ewes put together. Shy breeders, indeed!

Ewes carry their lambs for a few days short of five months, to the time when, hopefully, the hill grasses are beginning to grow. The following days are long for man and dog. On a full session over the hill, I would expect to have walked about 15 miles, climbing in the region of 6,000ft. Research study has shown that a sheepdog on the hill will easily cover 100 miles in a day's work. That equates to a dog scaling 30,000ft, the height of Mount Everest, at one go! Two hundred years ago, James Hogg, the famous Ettrick Shepherd, claimed that the whole mountain fastness of Scotland would not be worth sixpence, if it were not for the shepherd's dog. Still very true today.

When Bran came on the scene, I had a dog that could be sent to check out the unseen side of a hilltop. On any occasion he failed to re-appear and meet up with me, I would circle towards him and deal with the problem he had invariably come across. If I could not actually catch sight of him, I would ask him to bark, a dog with a voice is a very useful tool. Dust, on the other hand, had a pretty useful nose, one good enough to smell a rice pudding baking in Hanoi. I quickly lost count of the number of lost lambs she hunted out, many times completely on her own volition. In this highly mechanical age there is still only one way to properly lamb a hill, that is for a shepherd to pull on a pair of stout boots, pick up his cromach (crook) and walk out with a team of good dogs. No factory could ever manufacture a machine to do anything like it.

The shepherds of six adjoining hirsels, running along the north shore of Loch Katrine, worked as a team for five series of gatherings during the year. Always starting on the lowest ground, at the east end of the loch, each hirsel would be tackled in turn, finishing at Glengyle. In between times I competed at a few sheepdog trials, aiming to improve our performance season by season. The better your dog is on the trial field, the more use it will be working at home. Bran and his mother, Finn, herself a granddaughter of Chris, were the first of my breeding to lift top prizes. Finn won our first open trial trophy from a high quality field at Fintry. Invitations to put on sheepdog demonstrations followed, coming in from the length and breadth of Britain. My team appeared at both Stoke-on-Trent and Glasgow Garden Festivals, by which time we had a Subaru sponsored vehicle. Glasgow Festival was particularly challenging, as not only were we working with very lively Shetland sheep, but the arena was laid down with artificial turf – a surface the sheep obviously disliked. And they certainly couldn't eat it. They were, however, permitted to occasionally graze the lawns around the spectacular flower-beds, but only under the watchful gaze of my sheepdogs.

There were occasions when things went a bit pear-shaped. At Kelburn Castle, the stately home of Lord Glasgow, my sheep instantly took flight and could not get out of the ring fast enough. Led by a big, black, four-horned Hebridean tup, they scattered the crowd and stampeded through the castle grounds, vanishing into 80 acres of tall trees and dense undergrowth. My dogs eventually dug them out into the open and, helped by his Lordship, we herded them back to their trailer. The problem, as we later discovered, was the smell of fresh blood from countless bits of dead day-old chicks, dropped on the field by an inebriated falconer. It wasn't the demonstration I had intended, but it was very entertaining for the audience, for the short while it lasted.

I very much liked the look of a dog from Skipness, called Hemp, being run at trials by Alex McCuish. On an extremely wild

February day, the storm managing to rip off both windscreen wipers, I set off on a long and somewhat tricky drive down the Ardnamurchan Peninsula with Finn. Nine weeks later, my bitch delivered a litter of six, with one truly outstanding pup. Rees grew up to be a double of his great-great-great grandfather, Sheber, a Black and Tan sheepdog in all aspects. In the meantime, I had driven even further, back to the Gower Peninsula, collecting 12-month-old Kenneth from Colin Gordon at Stembridge Farm. From my earliest days working with dogs, my policy had been to keep a continuous line of closely related females, and bring in new and improving genetic traits through outsourced male lines. And so far, so good.

An exception to prove the rule was Kelly, who came into my hands as a rescue dog. A young lad from Wolverhampton had started out on the road to becoming a shepherd, and found it was a dream he was unable to follow through. His boots and crook he could take away with him to the city, but Wolverhampton is no place for a young collie used to running out on open hills. Reminiscent of my original Lassie, Kelly quickly settled in and was soon appearing in public as one of my exhibition team. The season usually began at the start of May, turning out for the charity fundraising event organised annually by Glasgow University Veterinary Medical Association. It was for GUVMA that I did my inaugural indoor sheepdog demonstration and, as a final decider of a competition they had been running, it was the first time my clients actually handled the dog for themselves. The more experienced dogs in my kennel were well used to working for other people, especially family members. At a gathering, there is no point in having extra bodies out on the hill if they haven't got a dog to work with. Another quote from James Hogg, 'A single shepherd and his dog will accomplish more in gathering a stock of sheep from any highland farm, than 20 shepherds without dogs.' A wise and perspicacious man, that Ettrick shepherd.

Even outdoors, space was sometimes at a premium. The most confined areas found us working around well-tended flowerbeds, on two occasions at Cambusbarron Park, Stirling, for their gala, and another time in the garden of Corstorphine Hospital, Edinburgh. Not all of the patients had been able to leave their beds to watch the display, so Bran was invited inside to do a proper ward-round for the others. There were many classroom visits to schools and colleges, which my dogs thoroughly enjoyed. Stardom came with a few pieces for television, although not *One Man and his Dog*. Channel 4 did a series about Christmas Day workers and wanted to include the routine of a shepherd. Lorraine Kelly and her crew filmed as I fed the hungry cows, before heading out to look over some of our sheep on the hill. Needless to say, the crew did not venture very far and it was pre-recorded well in advance of the day itself.

Bran had his five minutes of individual fame, on the radio. Steve Wright, on Radio 1, featured Bran counting sheep in Gaelic! As part of our sheepdog demonstrations, I would ask Bran to speak-up and count the sheep he had just penned, usually five or six. If he got it wrong, as occasionally happened, I would counter with the joke that Bran had been counting in Scotland's ancient tongue. This information had been relayed to the BBC in London. An invitation from our local radio station soon followed, to do a live interview. Little did I know what was in store. To ensure that there was no collusion, from a sealed envelope, a card with the word '*Seachd*' was drawn. I had not got a clue, my grasp of the language being almost non-existent. The correct pronunciation of *shech* came from the Gaelic speaking programme producer – and Bran barked seven times. We were spot on and got the thumbs-up from the technical crew behind the glass partition! I never quite worked that one out.

Over the years my dogs have opened a lot of interesting doors for me, initiating new and exciting projects. When André Goulancourt took over the Duke of Montrose's old hunting lodge, at Inversnaid, with stunning views across the northern end of Loch Lomond, it was to be developed into a Photographic Centre. With 50 acres/21ha of ground, Highland cattle and Shetland sheep were acquired to graze the vegetation, and double as photographic models. Not only did I help in the setting up and management of this enterprise, my sheepdogs were also in great demand in front of the cameras. As I herded the flock, the photography students were able to get a perfect collie's eye view of the sheep, and a sheep's eye view of sheepdogs at work.

Fergus Wood came on the scene with even bigger ideas. On his new farm at Kinlochard, small flocks of all ten native breeds of Scottish sheep would be set up. This was to become the nucleus of the concept of a Scottish Wool Centre, opened a few years later at Aberfoyle, designed to tell the entire story of wool. The fleece coming off the sheep's back was followed through to the extensive range of finished products. From her ten breeds, Scotland produces a wider range of wool than any other country in the world. A pound of Shetland wool, ideal for the finest knitwear, can spin into 19 miles of exquisite yarn. At the other end of the scale, thicker Blackface wool, used for carpets, hard-wearing tweed cloth and furniture upholstery, will only produce eight miles of spun fibre. The majority of Blackface wool is exported to Italy, and has been since the reign of David 1, to stuff into luxury mattresses. Over the centuries, many notable people throughout Europe must have been conceived on Italian mattresses stuffed with extremely comfortable Scottish Blackface wool.

I toured much of the country with Fergus, buying sheep for his enterprise, and overseeing the establishment of each flock at Ledard Farm. This provided a great deal of work for my dogs, and we soon began to appreciate that breeds not only looks different but will exhibit quite distinctive temperaments. Of all Scottish breeds, the Soay, originating from St Kilda, proved to be the most difficult for any dog to get to grips with. They could do everything except fly – and they made pretty good attempts to even do that. It was, however, all immense experience for man and dogs.

I am often asked how I became a shepherd. The answer to that is simple: I started with the right dog. A second question is much more difficult to unravel, the matter of training sheepdogs. A very large manual needed be written on that subject and, when the Scottish Qualifications Authority contacted me, that is exactly what I spent two years of my life trying to accomplish.

Tutor

CERTIFICATES ABOUND IN THE 21st century, every walk of life, it seems, leads to one diploma or another, and the more bits of paper the merrier. When, in 1998, the Scottish Qualifications Authority (SQA) discovered a bit of a gap in their syllabus, I was recruited to design a course in Sheepdog Handling and Management. A few meetings with SQA staff, Hamish Brad and Eleanor MacPherson at Hanover House, Glasgow, and I was up and running on the project, quickly having to master a whole new vocabulary of educational jargon. My own 'performance criteria' was to fully explain the subject in five 'units', a mammoth task in itself. Gill Simpson, a vet based in Edinburgh, worked with me on the Veterinary Care component, and only a vet or veterinary nurse can teach this unit to students. To achieve an SVQ (level 3) Certificate in Sheepdog Handling, four of the five units had to be successfully undertaken. With no time-limit, handlers could select their units to best fit around their individual requirements. Any student passing all five units would also receive a certificate from the International Sheep Dog Society, which has given the course full support.

The inaugural residential weekend session was held at Oatridge Agricultural College, West Lothian, in September 2000. Students enrolled from as far away as Northern Ireland and the remotest corner north-west of Scotland, and there was an even split between their backgrounds. One third just owned a collie and fancied the chance to work on sheep, mostly as an adjunct to the obedience and agility skills of their dogs. There were those who really wanted to find employment as shepherds and needed to hone the necessary skills. The final group were already farmers who, rather than engage a shepherd, wanted to learn how to properly handle a dog for themselves. Held every two months or so, the handlers had time between units to practise the techniques they had picked up at the college. And there was an awful lot to cover in the scheduled 17 hours and 30 minutes between Friday evening and Sunday afternoon.

Half of the time was spent with handlers and dogs in the lecture theatre, slotted in between practical working sessions in the field.

In dog terms, it is the choice of pup which is pivotal, whether buying from someone else or picking one from a home-bred litter. Even before reaching this stage, some thought should be given to the type of dog you are looking for, and the work you expect it to do. One of my students, Carol Johnston, had the foresight to enrol first and then acquire a suitable dog. Old English Sheepdogs are undoubtedly big and handsome, but not much use in herding wild sheep over mountain terrain. Similarly, you would not not want a rumbustious New Zealand Huntaway bringing dairy cows in for milking. Look around for dogs already doing the type of work you have in mind and source a puppy from there. Ideally you ought to see both parents going through their paces. With a home-bred litter, the parentage should be known, although this is not always the case.

In either situation, there will be one particular pup which will catch your eye. At this stage there are vital checks to be made, ensuring that there are no physical defects. Look for clear, bright eyes, with no signs of weeping; top and bottom teeth that meet evenly in the mouth – and no bad breath; clean skin and a glossy coat, especially beneath the tail. Signs of diarrhoea are bad news. Finally, feel the tummy area, which should not be tender or distended. This is the time to ask about any worming regime the puppy has been on. If you meet a negative response, begin one as soon as possible. Similarly, enquire whether any vaccinations have been given. If home-bred, you ought to be up to this point already. At about eight weeks, the pup is ready to leave mum and come into your personal care. From now on you are entirely responsible for the welfare of your puppy.

I cannot stress enough the importance of the next few hours. This is when a new puppy becomes bonded to you, transferring its maternal affinity to the human who, from now on, is the most important facet in its young life. Being carried inside a jacket is advantageous; body warmth and aroma both play a part in this process, as does hearing the steady rhythm of your heartbeat. This stage cannot be hurried, so be prepared to sit, or even lie down, until the pup thinks you are the best thing since sliced bread. Some hours spent in achieving a successful transfer of loyalty will be rewarded later.

Accommodation for the new puppy can range widely, from the comfort of a family kitchen to a pretty basic outhouse. The criteria, however, are the same; light, clean, comfortable and draught-free. At this age there won't even be the vestiges of toilet control, so floor space must be of the type easily wiped and cleaned. Any pup will always need to go outside quite soon after being fed. By being alert the puppy can be often lifted in good time and quickly carried outside, avoiding accidents. In all aspects of training, prevention is always better than cure. Praise should be given for toilet activity in the correct place and the pup will soon learn the routine. This, along with early answering to its name, and training has begun before you really know it.

Once settled in to its new surroundings, every puppy will learn a great deal for itself. Specialists in dog behaviour believe that puppies assimilate and retain more information between six and ten weeks old than at any other stage in life. Start with the maxim of encouraging behaviour you approve of, and discouraging traits you disapprove of. The degree of discouragement will depend entirely on the dog, some needing a stronger hand than others. Equally important is the way you socialise your pup, taking ample opportunity to meet people, especially children, and other dogs. There may be small animals and poultry around, but I would always keep a puppy well away from larger livestock until a later stage. Life for a young dog should be full of fun and things to do, but always in a safe environment. This is the time for building up confidence.

There are a number of diseases against which every

puppy ought to be vaccinated. Some immunity will have been derived from the mother's milk, but after weaning this quickly diminishes. First inoculation can be administered at around 11 weeks, followed a fortnight later by a booster. Two weeks later a pup's immunity will have peaked and can be maintained at this optimum level by constantly mixing with as many older dogs as possible. Fleas, lice and ticks can be a problem, and there will be a constant threat of round worm infestation. Fortunately, there are excellent proprietary remedies to treat all these afflictions. If in any doubt about the health or condition of your pup, seek prompt veterinary advice. Expensive, but it will be money well spent.

Puppies will begin to take solid food as soon as their eyes open and they begin to explore what the wider world has to offer. Initially they will paddle about in the food rather than eat it, but soon cotton on to the right idea. Feeding young puppies from the rim of an old fashioned milk churn will keep their feet out of the food. My ration is made up of a cooked flaked maize base, to which white fish meal and cod-liver oil have been added. Puppies prefer a moist feed, soaked in milk to provide a little extra in the way of calcium, vitamins and minerals. Dogs have very sensitive mouths, in the wild never devouring anything above blood heat, so offer the mash on the cool side. Three or four small feeds a day, as much as is readily cleared up. At four months, morning and evening feeds will suffice. I always have dry meal available on an ad-lib basis, along with a dish of clean water. This is the feeding regime for all my dogs. Long marrow bones, first cooked-off in an oven, are ideal for pups to chew, especially when they are changing their teeth. Keep young dogs clear of anything small enough to accidentally choke on. Safety first is the general rule.

Housing for working dogs is not always what it should be. Tim Longton, one of the best sheepdog handlers in England, once called at a farm where a pair of collies were tied up in the open, with no visible means of shelter. There had, at one time, been a stack of dried bracken standing in the middle of the farmyard, under which the two dogs adequately denned. But it had long gone. An extreme case, but by no means rare. The basic requirements are simple, water-tight and draught proof, but with plenty of light and fresh air – and a dry bed. Not too much to ask. A raised sleeping platform, about six inches (15cm) off the ground, would be even better. An outside run, especially one where a young dog can see what's going on, will keep the pup engaged and alleviate boredom. A range of buildings can easily be pressed into service, a section of a garage, a small loose box or redundant pig-sty. A few really lucky ones get to live in the house with the master, but make it a rule to forbid scrounging for food at the table. Such bad habits are difficult to break.

It is never too soon to get a puppy used to walking nicely on a lead, never allowed to be pulling ahead. Even though most working dogs will hardly ever see a lead, it is a useful facility to have. On the lead a puppy can be encouraged to walk to heel, a practice I maintained when my dogs were running loose. When the need arises, a lead-trained dog is always quite content to be left tethered.

Your puppy will answer to its name – most of the time. It is essential that this command is obeyed without it ever becoming a battle of wills. When reluctant to come, make a fuss over another dog and the pup will soon appear at hand. Another ploy is to sit on the ground and play with a piece of paper or handkerchief in your hands, curiosity will lead to the same result. It is best to avoid conflict. The sit command comes next, quickly followed by sit and stay, always speaking in a clear and firm tone. On the sit command, push the tail-end down with one hand while holding the other hand against the pup's chest, you will be in complete control. Give lots of praise and walk away, calling the pup as you go. Then repeat this simple exercise every few yards and, surprisingly quickly, the lesson will soon be learned. It is best to keep training sessions quite short, especially to begin with. Two or three times a day is far better than one long lesson. The stay component is all about timing, yours not the pup's. As you move your hand away from the young dog's chest, hold the other hand quite high, in front of the pup's face, telling it to stay. Back off slowly, and be prepared to call the pup to you before it lifts its rear end off the ground. Steadily widen the gap until, before too long, that lesson will have gone home. Distance will come through time.

By this time you should always be carrying a long stick of some description, a cromach (crook) if you have one, a shepherd's all important third leg and a useful extension of reach. The youngster will simply see this as an appendage of you, and for this reason it must never give a dog cause for alarm. Learning through play is always a bonus, reducing the number of lessons required at a later date. I know one or two dog handlers who make good use of a white football. A young dog, chasing a moving football, will instinctively want to pass the ball, either to the right or on the left side. If the pup elects for a right-hand pass, the 'Away to me!' command should be given, with 'Bye to me!' used for the left side. This is the first stage of putting sides onto your dog, and all done as part of a game. Some pups take to playfully rounding up hens but, apart from that, cannot do a lot more with them. Ducks, on the other hand are useful for training purposes, flocking and moving exactly as sheep – only many times slower. They do, however, possess the ability to fly, unless you keep the feathers on one wing well clipped. When Foot and Mouth disease brought livestock movement to a complete standstill, it was ducks to the rescue for those of us still needing to demonstrate our sheepdogs working in public. There was also the added bonus of duck eggs.

Geese can also double as sheep substitutes, and lay much larger eggs. The axiom of wing-clipping is the same as for ducks, as a friend of mine discovered to his cost. Booked to do a sheepdog demonstration at an agricultural show near Stirling, he had asked for local geese to be provided. After being grandly introduced to the crowd, half a dozen geese were released into the ring. Two dogs, well used to giving exhibitions with such birds, were sent away to gather the small flock. The lift at the far end of the arena was not quite what the handler expected. The dogs faultlessly fulfilled their role and began herding the birds towards their master. It was then that the geese lifted off the ground, flew once around the show-ground to get their bearings, and were last seen heading homeward. Collies are capable of many things but, as yet, flying is not among them.

Any time your young dog lies down, whether having gone around a ball, a flock of poultry or just settling down to rest, give that command. It does not matter if it is after the event, the dog will soon get the message. Further developments can be made by telling your dog to lie down and stay, while you walk on a little way. You will probably need to walk backwards at first, just to pre-empt any sneaking-up before you give the recall. By this time, to the verbal command to 'Come' can be added the same instruction by whistle. A dog will quickly become bilingual!

Your dog will soon happily stay put, until the moment you go out of sight. Now cunning strategy is required. Choose an open area with a gentle camber, lie the dog down and walk away backwards. The dog's eyes are only just above ground level, and you will quickly disappear over its horizon. You, with the advantage of height, will still see the dog long after he has lost sight of you. Dogs always get up by raising their front end first. As you see any elevation of the head, instantly, and very firmly, reiterate the lie down command. The ideal spot for you to stand is where the dog is actually out of your line of vision too, but any movement from the dog will bring the top of its head into view. It is very much the case of the dog not seeing you but, if it thinks about moving, you can see it. Later, this can be reinforced by the simple ploy of leaving the dog lying outside, while you are inside and have a clear and uninterrupted view through a window. When the dog shows any inclination to move, a rap on the glass through which you are watching is usually enough of a reminder. A starling, mimicking my recall whistle, once caused a bit of a problem. The dog concerned soon realised that it was really not me sitting up a tree or calling from a high wire!

I have confidently left trained dogs for hours at a time, outside lecture theatres, in the back of open vehicles, and loose in their whisky-barrel kennels at Garden Festivals. One afternoon, at the Glasgow Festival, I was cornered by a bunch of rather irate ladies telling me how cruel I was, keeping two poor dogs tied-up in their kennels for hours at a time. I edged away before their wrath until there was a good distance between us and the unfortunate hounds. At this point I called out Finn, who nosed her way through the milling crowd to my feet. Then I whistled for Bran, who appeared alongside me moments later. To say that the women were astounded would be an understatement. To finish my party piece in good style, I then asked my dogs to go back to their respective barrels. I explained that a dog tied by the neck is not a lot of use to a shepherd, especially in case of an emergency. Dogs can often come speeding to the rescue from quite a distance.

This was exemplified on another occasion at Glasgow, when a small Cashmere goat kid pulled off a Houdini act, squeezing itself out of its pen gate and leaving the building. Within seconds, the kid had been swallowed up by the hordes of visitors thronging the festival gardens. Witnesses later told me Finn and Bran went after the young goat, herding her back through a forest of legs, saw it safely delivered to the correct pen, and then returned to their kennels – entirely on their own volition.

Training a sheepdog to this standard requires time and dedication, neither of which can be skimped. Having reared your own young dog, or bought one ready to train, the limiting factor is the speed and endurance of that dog. It is also of paramount importance to have introduced the stop whistle, without exception handlers use a long, loud blast! A whistled command has much more force than a spoken one. Once the dog has shown a positive interest in sheep, usually between eight and ten months, formal training can commence. Although this is the norm, some pups demonstrate unmistakable interest much earlier and some dogs will do nothing for a couple of years. Strains of sheepdogs which are slow starters will often reward their handlers by having a longer working life. Welsh Black and Tans certainly fall into this category.

There are probably as many ways to train a working dog as there are dog handlers. The end result, however, is always the same, having an effective working partner at hand. This gets underway as soon as your young dog is able to pass and easily get in front of its sheep. Nothing upsets a novice dog more than sheep getting away and, believe me, hill sheep have a fair turn of speed. Bad habits picked up at this point, whining, barking and even gripping, can be difficult to eradicate. A dog that will bark on command, or take a good hold of a sheep, will pay dividends, but training for these attributes must come later. I begin lessons with only a few sheep, previously worked by an experienced sheepdog, in a small paddock with good stone dykes. Keep an older dog at hand to tidy things up when they go wrong, but never use a seasoned campaigner for training purposes. This is a lesson I learned very early in my career.

Ernie Rees had a great Black and Tan called Sheber, mentioned in an earlier chapter. Two of Sheber's pups, litter brothers, were kept and seemed to develop into carbon copies of their father. So Ernie was in the fortunate position of having three good working dogs at hand, until the gathering morning Sheber went out hunting rabbits instead. With two dogs still available to him, Ernie set off to Rhossili Down with hardly a care in the world. But, as soon as this gather of Welsh Mountain sheep got underway, neither of Ernie's promising young dogs would do a thing for him. Every command was steadfastly ignored because Sheber, from whom the young dogs actually took their cue, was not there to give the lead they were looking for. Always train dogs individually.

A classic example of natural instinct was demonstrated by a year old Border Collie, answering to Spud, who was introduced to sheep for the very first time at Oatridge. Spud's South African owner, then living in an Edinburgh suburb, had taken her dog to both obedience and agility classes, and was keen enough to enrol in the first ever sheepdog handling course. As the student residing closest to the agricultural college, Spud and his handler were roped into appearing in front of a television crew, to film a preview for Scottish News. With Kenneth and Bran, I had left 20 ewes standing in the middle of large, level field, my dogs lying well away from the sheep. Spud was walked on his lead, slowly approaching the small flock, all the time listening to encouraging words from his handler. As soon as Spud focused on his sheep, ears characteristically cocked, he was unleashed and enthusiastically shhhhushed away. Sweeping clockwise to the far side of his ewes, Spud dropped perfectly on command. Apart from lifting his tail into the air, a sure sign of a bit of uncertainty, it was a very satisfactory introduction to sheep. Asked to do it again, for take-two, there was absolutely no chance! But it was a confidence boosting start for both of them.

With a solid stone wall, failing that a secure fence-line, no matter how the sheep respond, a training exercise can be carried out. If your dog will not leave your side, the command will be to 'Walk up'. This instruction is used to drive sheep in a straight line – the actual direction does not matter in the least. Try and fall back, a little behind the dog, and eventually you will be able to stand still and let your dog work on unaided. If sheep face up to the dog, by walking up quietly, directly behind your collie, raising your arms to appear even larger to the sheep, they will usually give way. Hopefully your dog will not be aware of the extra assistance and confidence will be enhanced by success. Most sheepdogs will instinctively go to the head of its sheep, directly opposite to where the handler is standing. No matter which way you circle, your dog should adjust its position to balance the flock, always at 12 o'clock to the shepherd. Walk away and the flock should follow behind.

When your pupil flanks around the sheep, depending on which side, give the appropriate command. The conventional use of 'Bye' for left and 'Away' to the right has a practical application. A sheepdog out on an open hillside, with a force eight gale scattering words as they leave the shepherd's mouth, would be wondering whether that letter T, which just flashed past its left ear, was from lefT or righT. Dogs, however, seem to accurately differentiate between the commands Bye and Away. Working any dog is all about communication. Good hill dogs can easily, and often do, work at distances in excess of a mile.

Quite early, the recall and stop whistles will have been established. A whistle always makes more of an impact on your dog, having greater force than a vocal command. So fine tuned, a dog has the ability to hear a ticking watch at forty paces. Now is the time to add your flanking left-hand and right-hand whistles, which will give you four out of the five commands you will need. The last whistle is for the 'Walk up' directive, maintaining a straight line irrespective of where the handler is positioned. Driving is, without doubt, the most onerous of the disciplines, running contrary to the natural inclination of a sheepdog to bring sheep directly towards the handler. I know of a couple of sheepdog trainers who, especially for candidates destined for trials, actually concentrate on the driving element from the beginning. Any dog failing to fully master the drive will struggle at sheepdog trials. They will, of course, be more than adequate at everyday shepherding.

Gael was one of my best driving dogs. This little Black and Tan bitch could be left in charge of a cut of sheep and, all on her own, would drive them steadily all the way home to the fank. When a hill is gathered, the best part of 800 ewes and between June and September all the lambs to go with them, would be gathered together. This is far too big a bulk of sheep to move in one go, so shepherds would pair off and take away their share or cut of the flock, a smaller number being far easier to work with. Gael gave me the option of further reducing the numbers in the cut I was herding, happily bringing along her packet of sheep behind us. The most amazing thing was Gael never seemed to have any of the difficulties my colleague and I found ourselves dealing with, mainly intransigent lambs frantically trying to get back to the hill.

The most difficult of the gathers is at the June lamb-marking, which will be the first experience lambs will have of being rounded up and taken off their ground. Sheep in the Borders will have had the advantage of being herded morning and evening, dogs working them down early in the day and turning them up again for the night. Hirsels there are usually gathered heft by heft, in manage-able numbers, and with lambs already used to the ways of sheepdogs. Things are quite different in the Highlands. Hirsels are gathered en masse, with lambs that haven't a clue as to what is happening. Lambs, reluctant to leave the familiar surroundings of their own ground, are soon left behind by the older sheep well accustomed to the proceedings. Shepherds and their dogs must endeavour to keep everything together. If a group of lambs break away, instinctively heading back to where they started from, even the most experienced sheepdogs will have their work cut out to resolve the situation. The hefting instinct of sheep is immensely strong, each hill ewe lambing within a few feet of where she had come into this world. If sheep ever escape from a gather, they will inevitably try it again and again. It is rumoured that elephants inherited their very long memory from sheep.

A rather decrepit, bare-skinned Border Collie came into my hands. Registered as Chieftain, his master had retired from shepherding through ill health and, although his kennel mates had found alternative employment, nobody wanted to take on old Craig. Practically blind, and totally deaf, I never saw a collie that was better at handling a group of runaway lambs. On one notable occasion I was coming in with the last sheep off a neighbouring hirsel, all the renegades from the cuts in front of us had joined our ranks, greatly swelling the number of lost lambs for us to handle. As the head shepherd and I tried to coax our charges through a gate and into the relative safety of a well-fenced park, Craig kept the entire left flank moving steadily forward, calmly facing down every potential break of lambs. Meanwhile, Iain Campbell and I really had our work cut out to deal with the foment on the right. We still had time, though, to marvel at Craig's innate driving ability, senile or not.

A few nights later Craig slept away peacefully. It was sad, even though he had only been with me a very short time. I laid the old warrior to rest in the ground where he had herded his last flock, wrapped snugly in one of their soft, comfy fleeces. His trials in this life were finally at an end.

When bringing on young dogs, lessons conducted in secure surrounds can lay down firm foundations, but there is no substitute for getting out on the open hill for practical sheep herding. My usual team would consist of four dogs, a top dog (not necessarily the number one dog) to deal with specialist duties, two gofers to do most of the running, and a novice. As long as a young dog will stop and stay on command, it is better to take it out for experience – a dog learns nothing if left in a kennel. My dogs always walk to heel. There are several valid reasons for this; safety, if there is traffic in the vicinity; to conserve their energy; because of lines of sight. Standing taller than my sheepdogs, my horizon is that much further away and I can see far more ground than they can. Remember, though, their hearing and sense of smell are far, far superior to those of humans. Apart from acute hearing, a dog's sense of smell will allow it to identify one or two single molecules out of a trillion others. It is vital that, through training, we do not suppress a young dog's ability to utilise these natural powers, and do everything possible to stimulate full use of initiative. Teach a dog through respect and encouragement and they will reward you with a lifetime of true diligence and loyalty.

A further step in augmenting a young sheepdog's development is to enter a few trials, but be aware that some dogs react quite differently when out in public. Finn was a classic example of this, perfectly behaved at home, an absolute terror on a sheepdog trial course. In her early days, she would hit her packet of sheep like an Exocet Missile! Even after eventually taking her first stop whistle at the top of the field, her antics were not quite finished. We still had a few more early retirements before things finally settled down. In the final tally, Finn took home more silverware than any other of my dogs. Her forte was penning and I seldom failed to shut the gate on her sheep.

A sheepdog trial course is set out to present the handler and dog with the tasks of everyday herding. From the moment you set foot inside the rope, total concentration is essential, even to the way you walk out to the starting post. The judge will usually be based in a vehicle, directly in line with the fetch element which finishes at the handler's post. By approaching your starting position along that axis, the dog will know exactly where to find the sheep – even if they are out of sight. Place your dog on the side you wish it to run, which is entirely optional. The further back you tell the dog to wait will be an indication as to how far away the sheep will be waiting. All this crucial information is being imparted to your dog before you have even started the trial.

The clock starts ticking as soon as the dog begins its outrun and, at that point, you will have full marks on the scorecard. Points are deducted by the judge for anything less than perfection. On the outrun, a dog should gradually widen out, to pass behind the sheep without disturbing them. Next comes the all-important lift, the first contact between dog and sheep, done smoothly and with the sheep on the fetch line. This should be kept as straight as possible. A pair of gates about halfway down the course, set seven yards apart, give the judge and spectators a good idea as to how the work is progressing. The fetch finishes at the handler's post, and it is important to move away slightly to the left, allowing the sheep to be kept on that line. Passing the post to their right-hand side, a triangular drive will take the sheep 45° to the left (unless it is an anticlockwise set-up), through another set of gates. A sharp turn, hard to the right, the sheep hopefully keeping to the cross-drive line and through the final gates. From there it should still be a direct line along the third leg of the triangle to the pen. Many a handler, making his way from post to pen, loses concentration here, letting the sheep drift a little and dropping a few precious points.

At home, once you have gathered sheep you will need to put them in somewhere. On the trial park, the idea is to put your small packet of sheep into a free-standing pen. At this juncture the pen will look very small, and the sheep will have no intention of willingly going into it. And all the while the clock is counting down. Penning often turns into a war of attrition but, if you can keep sheep and dog settled, they will mostly oblige. JM Wilson MBE once told me that if your sheep are standing still, not going in any of the umpteen wrong directions, then you are winning the battle. No sooner have you closed the gate of the pen, you are asking the dog to turn them out again. The final task is to either shed off a single sheep, or evenly split the group into two. Your dog must be in full control of the sheep you are left with. When the judge is fully satisfied with the single or shed, the clock stops and your trial is over. Most times the clock will beat the competitors, although points remaining on completed sections will still count towards the potential prizes at the end of the day.

Judging is always likely to be contentious. Where and for what reasons should points come off? JM Wilson, who had more perfect scores than any one else, gave me a great deal of erudite guidance in this matter. Using the outrun as an example; a dog stopping a bit short of its sheep, then moving on without a command, should still be docked a touch. If whistled-up to complete the outrun, that would be penalised more, leaving full points for any sheepdog covering the waiting sheep without any intervention from the shepherd. The winner of nine Supreme and two Brace International

Championships, to be added to a tally of 11 Scottish National single and six Brace titles, JM Wilson maintained that a perfect run was not possible. Running Glen at Edinburgh in 1956, he put his own hypothesis severely to the test. A click of his fingers sent Glen away, and not a word or whistle was to be heard, or a murmur from the large crowd, until the sheep came to JM's feet at the end of the fetch element. It will not come any better than that. A master class, indeed.

A few thoughts on judging. I use a system favoured by Jimmy Millar, A4 sheets with a printed plan of the trial course. Starting as a judge's clerk, my job was to pencil in the exact route taken by the dog, listening as I was told to mark the deductions at the precise location and specify the nature of indiscretions. At the end of each run the points retained would be written at the top of the page, alongside the name of the competitor and dog. Score sheets were filed in order of merit as we went along, the dog currently leading at the top, providing a full set of results as the last handler left the field. In the event of a tie, the dog with the better outbye work, over outrun, lift and fetch, would get the nod, otherwise a rerun will be required.

Any time a handler wanted to come and discuss how I had seen the run, and find out where points had been lost, I was able to immediately pull out the relevant sheet. One competitor, wondering where he had dropped so many points off his outrun, could see the tell-tale pencil line passing right in front of his feet. At the very start his dog had actually crossed the course and been deducted half the outrun points. This was a fundamental handling error; all would have been well if the dog had changed sides by passing behind the competitor. In the days before modern technology, to have such evidence in black and white was often invaluable.

Sheepdog trials certainly help in Personal Development Plans of both handler and dog, widening the experience of both. They are also great social gatherings. At the higher echelons, trials become more complex and are run over much longer courses. Although the time-limit will be adjusted accordingly, the speed at which the sheep are expected to cover the course will still be around a steady 3mph. Over the years Bo, Bran and Finn all won trials for me, but

I still hold that Finn finishing in fourth place at Bennachie was our best ever achievement. Run over the flanks of a notable 1,733ft/528m Aberdeenshire landmark, this was a double-lift trial, dogs coming halfway in with one packet of sheep before being turned back to a different area to lift a second group. This should be well within the capability of a good hill dog, one used to being redirected whilst at its everyday work. On unfamiliar ground, and with strange sheep, this can prove to be quite a challenge.

Displays and demonstrations provide ample opportunities for explaining exactly how and why we train our sheepdogs and why, along with boots and cromach, they are all a shepherd will really need. Working regularly with feisty Shetland sheep at the Scottish Wool Centre, Aberfoyle, I was able to demonstrate the different stages of a sheepdog's development. The sheep would immediately take refuge on a ridge, situated in front of the cafeteria, the elevation making them look larger to the dog. The approaching sheepdog would also appear somewhat smaller to the sheep. Animal psychology at work. Visitors enjoying their refreshments would have a ringside seat for the action.

Starting with a young and inexperienced dog, the Shetlands would be quite prepared to stand their ground, even stamping their front feet in defiance, as the collie approached. Stopping an adolescent Kelly well short of the sheep, not asking her to attempt a task beyond her present capability, the young bitch would be returned to the Subaru estate. Then I would call out Kenneth, a more experienced dog, walking him up quite slowly. Before this sheepdog had even padded halfway to the sheep, all defiance evaporated, they obligingly filed down into the arena. This was a good illustration of the 'eye' or natural power a good working dog will exude, an ability to move any livestock without undue fuss. Sheep of the Shetland breed, and a few others, will not only defy a weak or uncertain dog, they have been known to actually chase the intruder. Sheep also have very long memories, Once defeated, a dog may never gain ascendancy over those particular animals.

At the penning stage, people spectating would soon appreciate that the instruction to lie down is very much a movable feast. Whether spoken or whistled, entirely depending on the tone or note of urgency, it can mean anything between slow-down-a-bit, and come-to-a-dead-stop in a horizontal position. The final element would be to use the best dog at hand to shed-off a particular ewe, as if we were out on the open hillside and not a pen in sight. At lambing time, to come across a sheep with two heads is a shepherd's worst nightmare. The head at the front is no great problem, although it is usually filled with mischief and ploys to outwit man and dog. It is the head at the rear end, peeking out from under the tail, that is the cause for concern. A dog is needed to face up that ewe, taking a firm hold if necessary, allowing the shepherd to move in and render essential assistance.

Demonstrations and trials are all very good, but the sheep are seldom out of sight. On the hill, however, sheepdogs are frequently working on unseen sheep, well out of the handler's vision. In these circumstances, the dogs have to assess the situation and act accordingly – without any input from the shepherd. This is exactly why training must never quell a sheepdog's inbred initiative, or the ability to think and work things out for itself. My dogs could well do their job without me, I could never work sheep without them.

Some sheepdog handlers avoid all the trials and tribulations of rearing and training a new member of the team, taking the more expedient route of buying a dog fully trained. These, however, do not come cheap. Even then, there will be an all important bedding-in period as man and dog get used to each other's foibles and establish lines of communication. I once bought in a Welsh Black and Tan, as much for breeding purposes as his working ability, only used to hearing his native language. I quickly learned to whistle in Welsh and he soon began to listen in English. All through his life, especially when under pressure, a command from me would occasionally go unheeded and I would have to remind my dog to listen in the appropriate language. Bi-lingual or not, a sheepdog can acquire a pretty comprehensive vocabulary. Chaser, a Border Collie studied at Wofford College, South Carolina, can understand 1,022 words, claimed as a world record for a non-human animal.

A well-trained dog will give many years of service and, providing they are given ample opportunity, will continue to develop throughout their working life. For just food and board a dog will give you a lifetime of service. My dogs were always kennelled together for social interaction, with two compartments available for any required separation of males and females. At some point, an alpha dog will inevitably lose domination over the team, not just slipping one or two places down the hierarchy but being reduced to lowest status. With extra care and individual attention, such dogs still have much to offer, even in the twilight of their days.

The ultimate loss of a much valued and faithful companion is always hard to bear and, even with many years' experience, it never gets any easier. Whilst being a severe critic of the fees veterinary surgeons are charging today, I must admit that the range of services on offer has greatly increased. Janet Thomas, a vet based in Oldham, pioneered an invaluable pet bereavement support service, which is ever more widely available. Thomas heads an advisory group for the Society for Companion Animal Studies (SCAS), who make bereavement support accessible through The Blue Cross organisation. Even the hardest of hearts will crack at times like this.

It has been the greatest of privileges to have herded sheep over mountains and moorland, with my sheepdogs ever at my side. I have also been able, in a small way, to have helped a few others by providing sheepdogs with good working potential, and passing on the skills and knowledge I managed to accumulate from so many friends and colleagues. The principal and staff at Oatridge Agricultural College were both enthusiastic and supportive of the aims and outcomes laid down in my SQA course in Sheepdog Handling and Management. When Laura Cunningham, a former student, was a member of the triumphant Scottish team, winning the 2006 televised series of *One Man and His Dog*, it could be considered a job well done.

Laura and her equally enthusiastic Blue Merle dog, Loeki, had been amongst my first intake of students in September 2000. Although coming from a non-agricultural background, Laura Cunningham is now well noted for her dogs, working them with a flying-flock of Shetland sheep, moving from place to place to graze

Scottish Wildlife Trust reserves in an environmentally friendly fashion. The ancient craft of men and women herding livestock with their dogs is surely safe in the hands of the next generation.

Theory

IT IS WELL KNOWN that dogs evolved from wolves but, judging from the latest DNA evidence, it would appear that the process could have started 100,000 years earlier than was once thought. This being the case, the bond between man and dogs is a very old one indeed. Way back in the mists of time, nomadic man would have been a hunter/gatherer, living in small groups and constantly on the move. Eking out a living as best they could, these early people were constantly surrounded by danger. Large predacious animals prowled over the landscape, and when your neighbours came to call, they were not coming for afternoon tea. Man, as dirty a creature then as he is now, would always be leaving scraps and debris that would be bound to attract wild, camp-following dogs. If these rather nebulous dogs could give a successful early warning of impending danger, they would have been well rewarded for their services. Morsels of red meat would have been a welcome change from a diet of leftovers.

Making food available has always been a sure-fire way of bonding with animals, especially dogs. So long ago, in those indeterminate times, the main food supply for both man and his new

best friends was never in one place for long. Herds of grazing animals would follow the path of the sun during the spring and summer, retracing their steps for the coming winter. In the northern hemisphere, as the icy grip of winter took hold, there would be a short lull in the almost constant migration. Unlike fresh water, the sea can remain open and unfrozen, providing valuable sources of food through the cold, dark winter months. Early archaeologists were intrigued by the enormous mounds of sea shells, which served to identify these very ancient campsites. Respite was brief and, as the days lengthened, the annual migration would once more be under way.

To maximise the efficiency of any hunt for fresh food, every available member of the group would have been pressed into service. Even then, success could often prove elusive. When a kill was made, the camp-following dogs would have been close behind to avail themselves of anything left over. Although probably not far removed from the original *Canis lupus*, the grey wolf, there was now a strain of wild dog forging a commensal relationship with man, to the mutual advantage of both parties. At this distance, it is not possible to attribute a date to this momentous and ultimately life-changing union. Latest research, however, places this alliance firmly in the Palaeolithic Period, a time leaving us chipped and unpolished stone tools, and very little else. A few hearthsites and evidence of butchered wild animals help to retrace the faint footsteps of our remote ancestors.

Even in those long lost days, dogs would have learned quickly and soon began to modify their behaviour. Rather than simply following on to a tribal hunt, some still wild dogs began to get actively involved. This greatly increased the chances of success. By being present at the point of kill, the dogs would have the reward of fresh blood and warm meat, a considerable improvement on cold offal and throwaway scraps. In turn, man was soon out hunting with fewer bodies, but assisted by dogs. It still would have been rather haphazard, although undoubtedly an improvement. Those not taking part in the hunt would then have more time to forage for roots, nuts, fruits, fungi and insects, and also to devise ways of preserving the increased supply of meat. Flesh would have been sun-dried, smoked and, if it was available, salted. Some was stashed in peat bogs, possibly as a safeguard against times of shortage. In the service of man, dogs had added hunting skills to their guarding duties.

Migration would continue for a long time to come. Apart from a winter break, man was always on the move, never in one place for more than a small number of days. But all the while, hunting techniques were gradually being refined. The most basic and somewhat brutal method was to use the dogs to stampede their intended prey over a precipice. This resulted in an indiscriminate slaughter, killing far more animals than they could possibly utilise. Even with the ability to conserve a good quantity of the spoils, it was ultimately wasteful. More selective was to run their quarry into a dead-end gully, where the choicest animals could be picked out and killed off. To achieve this, the hunters and their dogs had to be able to chase the herd in a predetermined direction. All round, skill levels were being improved, along with the first vestiges of herding.

Vertical cliffs and handy gullies are not always close at hand, especially on vast stretches of open grassland. The next major advancement seems to have been independently developed on quite separate parts of this planet – dig a deep hole and cunningly cover it. The implements used in the excavations would have still been primitive, but the hunting technique had become sophisticated. It was now essential to direct the intended victims precisely towards the camouflaged pit. There were probably more failures than successes, but herding dogs had indeed arrived. A massive change of lifestyle was not long in coming.

Many a long mile man had tramped, following in the hoofprints of his mobile larder. With the realisation that each point on the migration route would be passed twice in the succession of seasons, our forefathers must have been wondering why. At some important point in history, dogs were used to separate and hold onto a relatively small number of the migrating herds. Judging that they had enough animals to sustain themselves until herds retraced their steps, the rest of the herbivores could wander on in search of fresh pastures. For the first time, man could establish permanent settlement and forsake their long-established wandering ways. With this sedentary mode of life, man had much more time to spend developing new skills and crafts. Great improvements were made in tools, weapons and everyday utensils. Artwork and more skilful designs began to be applied to everyday accoutrements. Sometime around 125,000 years ago, civilisation first began to take root.

Without a doubt, this sea change was brought about by dogs' affinity for mankind. And this was still only the beginning. Having settled at a permanent location, the now domesticated livestock rapidly devoured the surrounding vegetation. Herding dogs would move the grazing animals to fresh pastures and keep them from straying away. Other dogs would be used to guard both animals and homestead from marauding predators and hostile humans. Hunting expeditions would still be undertaken, picking off any likely prey in the vicinity. By this stage, there would have been distinct lines developing from *Canis lupus*, the common ancestor of all dogs. Domestic dogs, kept as pets, have ever since provided companionship, and added a further line of security. On cold nights the body warmth of dogs would have been comforting, and the simple action of stroking pets reduced stress. Grooming also reinforces bonding between man and dog.

Only a few of the species held back from the migrating herds would have adapted well to their new existence, some dying off, others escaping. Animals of the camel, goat and cattle families seem to have prospered and soon produced fully-domesticated generations. Husbandry of pigs, sheep and poultry began in the Far East and eventually spread across to Europe. Faced with the problem of livestock overgrazing, specialist herdsmen and their dogs wandered widely in search of fresh pasture. Once the grassland had recovered, the flocks and herds could return, establishing the practice of rotation. As his expertise in land management increased, man would have noted that some strains of grass recovered from being romped by hungry mouths more rapidly than others. Seeds collected from such grasses would have been carefully collected and scattered over less productive areas. Not only were our ancestors managing their animals, they were also husbanding the land.

As a few strains of grass were developed into more productive cereals, and other arable crops were also introduced, the control of marauding animals became crucial. Long before the use of walls, hedges or fences to protect the valuable growing plants, both domestic stock and wild animals had to be kept away. One strain of *Canis familiaris* (domestic dog) maintained the original role of watchdog, a service many breeds still provide to this day. Overnight, livestock could be safely contained in stockades. By day, the animals would be taken away by the stockmen and their herding dogs, keeping them at a safe distance from the cultivated crops. Sometimes, particularly in summer, the grazing animals were taken quite far afield, often staying out for many weeks. The high hills and mountain pastures were favourite grazing grounds, sufficiently removed from ripening harvest at home. This form of transhumance is practised today in many countries, still following ancient routes. Twice a year the traffic in Madrid comes to a standstill as flockmasters and their sheep persist in exercising their inalienable rights of passage.

Outlying livestock had to be both close-herded and protected by the herdsmen's dogs, now showing distinct morphological changes. Lighter and more nimble dogs were undoubtedly selected by man as being more suitable for herding purposes. Physically larger and strongly aggressive dogs would serve in protective duties. Some of the evolving breeds kept to the middle ground, equally adept in a dual capacity. Household-companion dogs tended to have quite quickly been reduced in size, as at that time living space was small and crowded. Small dogs fulfilled their own functions in the service of man, particularly the control of vermin. Long-coated lap dogs could provide an added source of warmth, especially welcome for cold fingers. Very small dogs could even be used for personnel protection, and not only by barking and biting ankles. Some rather specialised dogs could be secreted beneath clothing, not only for comfort, but to take an assassin's knife. Oriental potentates and nobles would frequently conceal life-saving Pekingese under their elaborate robes.

The earliest permanent human settlement discovered so far is in Oman, southern Arabia, dating back some 125,000 years. Dr Jeffrey I Rose, University of Birmingham, has been investigating this ancient site, at Wādī 'Aybūt, Dhofar, founded at a time when *Homo sapiens* still shared this planet with Neanderthal man. In European terms, a settlement site at Mladeč, Czech Republic, has a 39,000 year history. Even closer to home, a Mesolithic transit camp has been identified at Biggar, South Lanarkshire, briefly occupied 14,000 years ago. At Cramond, just east of Edinburgh, the oldest British remains of an established settlement, 10,400 years old, has been uncovered. In County Derry, overlooking the River Bann, the Mount Sandel site has seven circular huts and a 9,000 year timeline. Constructed from woven saplings and originally covered with hides, six have a 6m/19ft diameter and a central hearth. The other is only 2m/7ft across, with an external hearth. With no animal enclosures or storage buildings, this Irish location was most probably of a temporary nature. Modern man seems to be equally at home either in permanent settlement or on the move with his dogs and livestock. Neanderthal man died out about 28,000 years ago, never having mastered the all important ability to work with dogs.

Settlement and civilisation led very quickly to the acquisition of wealth, certainly for the acknowledged leaders of any tribe or group. Prosperity was not a matter of accumulating treasure in the form of shiny metal artefacts, it depended entirely on the value of their domestic livestock – especially cattle. As late as the 18th century, transactions in the Highlands of Scotland were largely conducted in black cattle, a practice known as 'blackmail'. Across swathes of Northern Africa, camels are still considered to be a legitimate form of currency. The importance of animals led to marked improvements and through selective breeding the development of distinctive breeds. Today, in Britain, there are 26 breeds of cattle and 61 breeds of sheep native to these islands, to which many more European varieties have been recently added. From earliest times, successive waves of invaders to these shores have introduced new species and bloodlines to augment indigenous stock.

The ability of man to actively manipulate the evolution of his domestic animals, positively selecting for desired traits, is well recorded in the *Book of Genesis*. Jacob, grandson of Abraham, lived in the Middle East, somewhere around 1800BC. In order to marry

Rachel, the younger daughter of Laban, Jacob had to first marry Leah, the somewhat plainer older sister. Having worked for 14 years to get his heart's desire, Jacob was all for leaving the service of his father-in-law. Laban, however, was prepared to negotiate, quite desperate to retain the exemplary stockmanship of his best herdsman. A deal was struck whereby Jacob would claim for himself any sheep or goats from Laban's stock with white spots or speckles. Those being by far the small number, Laban believed that he had the better of the arrangement. Jacob sent his newly acquired animals away with his own shepherds and goat minders, staying with his two wives to tend Laban's stock for a further six years.

Jacob had hatched a very cunning plan. Each year, as the breeding season approached, Jacob and Laban's herdsmen took their animals to a poor and arid pasture, where there were only a few watering places. Around each waterhole, an enclosure was constructed from withes of poplar, almond and plane trees, from which the bark had been stripped. A ram and he-goat were separately tethered inside each of the paddocks, to service Laban's entirely dark-coated females as they came to drink. The exposed white wood, and the whitest sand scattered within the mating areas, would exert a strange and quite unexpected influence. Many of the resulting offspring were born with varying degrees of white fibres on their pelt. There would be no argument, any animal with even the smallest white dot belonged to Jacob. That was the agreement Laban had willingly accepted. Jacob prospered at Laban's expense; white fibre is far more valuable than any other, having the ability to take a range of colouring dyes. This is the earliest record of genetic engineering.

The story resumes in the early years of the 20th century. A farmer with a single pair of horses, a mare and a gelding, noticed that no matter what colour of stallion the mare was mated to, the resulting foal was always identical to her stable mate. When, after several years, the gelding was replaced with another of quite different hue, the colour of the new-born foal now matched that of the dam's neutered new ploughing partner. With this information, an agricultural college set up a research project. A number of black cows were individually housed in totally white surrounds, fed only on white feed, and had an outside view of a white bull in a white paddock. Hooded when mated, each female was serviced by a black bull of her own breed. Nine months later, calves carrying a surprising amount of white markings arrived on the scene. These cases, known as 'autosuggestion' have been reported in the journal of the Rare Breeds Survival Trust.

Considerable wealth could be accrued from livestock. White wool from sheep and white cashmere fibre, the ultra-fine undercoat of goats, were in constant demand. Milk, meat, hides and bones all added to the overall prosperity. Weight for weight, if burned on a fire, animal bones have a greater calorific value than coal. None of this would have been at all possible without a gamut of dogs, tireless in the service of mankind. In Great Britain and Ireland alone, we have 51 of the 130 breeds granted Championship status by the English Kennel Club. Domesticated livestock diversified into distinct breeds, to be best suited to the climate, terrain, vegetation and market demands of a particular area. The dogs needed to assist in tending these animals would have been bred to exactly fit the bill. The strongly built Old English Sheepdog was developed in the West Country, well able to herd breeds of large sheep, such as the Cotswold. Both these animals have graced these shores from ancient times, the sheep dating from as far back as the Roman occupation. In contrast, the relatively small Shetland Sheepdog was far more adept at dealing with the lighter and very agile island sheep, working them over largely rugged and rocky coastal terrain.

With the demise of the last major predator in Britain, a wolf claimed to have been shot by Iain MacQueen in 1743, the need to have dogs to guard British herds and flocks has diminished. Whether the last wolf met its end in the upper reaches of the Findhorn River or not, it is to mainland Europe we have to look for dogs still actively protecting their charges against predators and thieves. The Maremma is the best known of Italian sheepdogs, imposing in appearance, sturdy and brave, without being at all overly aggressive. The rapid rise in rural crime has led to an increased interest in this particular breed from both sides of the Atlantic. Chapter Ten will look at the many individual breeds of sheepdogs and collies, and their wide range of working abilities, in much more detail.

The adaptation of wild, camp-following dogs, starting as an effective alarm system, through hardy hunting accomplices to skilful herding companions, led directly to the civilisation of man.

Research

THEORY, EVEN BACKED UP by archaeology and scientific research, needs to be supported by documentation. Records of dogs go back a very long way, with several references dated to around 4,000BP (Before Present). When Abram is mentioned in the Old Testament, chapter 13 of the *Book of Genesis*, the Hebrew texts tell of the great herds of camels, cattle and oxen, large flocks of sheep and goats, and the dogs of the flocks. There is nothing more, other than God promoted Abram by changing his name to Abraham and setting him up as the patriarch of His chosen race. Later, Job (chapter 30, verse 1) makes a fleeting mention of the dogs of his flocks. About the same time, further east, Chinese chronicles noted the use of specialised dogs in the hunting of wild animals. Symbolic Feng Shui fu dogs (Foo Dogs) were placed watching doorways, to keep out evil spirits and keep the people safe.

Dogs were venerated in the Orient, and also used in ritual practices. There was a very early deity, depicted in the form of a dog, to whom dog sacrifices were made. Blood of specially raised dogs was ceremonially used in the swearing of covenants between Chinese nobles. The Mesopotamians, an ancient kingdom between the Tigris and Euphrates rivers, also invoked the blood of dogs for sealing oaths. In the Zhou Dynasty (1110–256BC), the Quanrong people went even further, believing themselves to be actually descended from a pair of great white dogs, worshipping their celestial canine ancestors. The Dog is one of the 12 divisions of the Chinese astrological calendar, and all dogs have their official birthday on the second day of the Chinese New Year. Some dogs were buried in expensive lacquered coffins, their necks often adorned with bells, clappers (called ling), or neck-rings made from silver and gold. Less fortunate dogs were eaten as food.

Associated with hunting alongside man, from very early times the Han Dynasty (206BC–220AD) appointed royal officers to oversee the breeding, selection, raising and training of the very best hunting dogs. Under the rule of Emperor Han Wu Ti, in the 2nd century BC, Confucianism became a widespread philosophy and China achieved unprecedented wealth and power. Enormous advances were made in both culture and technology, porcelain and paper being developed in this period. However, it was the duty of each and every keeper of the court kennels to bring out the finest hunting dogs on the planet. On this alone did the prestige of any Emperor stand or fall.

Early scholars of Arabia studied the night sky, seeing amongst the stars a hunter and his hunting dog. The Greek astronomers referred to the constellation as Orion and his companion was called Sirius – the Dog Star. Steadily padding from east to west at the hunter's heel, across the night skies of winter, Sirius shines with 23 times the luminosity of the sun, by far the brightest star visible from earth.

Hinduism, originating some 5,000 years ago, is the traditional religion of India and Nepal. While the ancient Greeks had ferocious Cerberus, a dog with three heads, guarding the gates of Hell, Hindu texts tell us that it is the entrance to Heaven which is constantly protected by a pack of dogs. In the Koran, Muhammad places dogs for home protection, hunting and herding livestock above all other dogs. Information passed down through oft-told stories or archaic texts can provide a pretty broad outline of our long history. Science, though, is able to fill in the picture in very precise detail. Spearheading this advance is radiocarbon dating from archaeological sites, and mitochondrial DNA analysis of animal remains. The resultant data is interesting and surprising.

A feature in the *Science* journal, June 1997, published a summary of the research carried out by Carles Vila et al, on the evolution of dogs from wolves. Taking information collected at 27 localities worldwide, details of 162 wolves and 140 dogs were evaluated. From 67 different breeds of dog, and the sample of wolves, there was sufficient diversity shown within both *Canis familiaris* and *Canis lupus* to form a significant conclusion. This was that there was enough evidence to support the hypothesis that wolves were indeed the ancestors of all domestic dogs. Other studies have narrowed the range further, to genes from only three grey she-wolves. The point of divergence has been pushed back, to a time more than 100,000BP.

The earliest sign of domestication in a dog was found at the Goyet Cave, in Belgium, the snout distinctively shortened – although not by much. This skull fragment has been dated to 31,700BP. Not too far away, in time and distance, cave paintings at Chauvet, France, depict a range of animals, including bears and dogs. As bears disappeared from that area around 29,000BP, we have an earlier date by 3,000 years, than those recovered from human and dog remains on that site. Neanderthal man dropped off the evolutionary tree around this time, although one per cent to four per cent of the purely Eurasian genome indicates evidence of interbreeding with modern man. Dr Peter Parham, Stanford Medical School, California, places these nuptials between 90,000 and 65,000 years ago. Ukraine has recovered traces of large and medium size dogs from a site at Mezhirich, with the relatively recent date of 15,000BP. A millennium later, the earliest known man/dog burial took place at Bonn-Oberkassel, Germany. With vast tracts of northern Europe still frost-bound, the last Ice Age not finally retreating until 10,000BP, man and his animals were content to inhabit warmer climes of the south.

A plethora of settlements in Germany, Switzerland, France and Spain yielded a great many remains of small dogs – household pets. The dates recovered from these sites range from 15,000 to 12,500BP. Brought to light from the sea-cut Danger Cave, on the western edge of the state of Utah, is the earliest ritual burial of dogs in the Americas. Elsewhere, Adam R Boyko et al have published a great deal of information from Neolithic sites at Jiahu, Henan Province, China. Covering the period 7,000–5,800BP, there is evidence of people growing rice, keeping pigs, and fermenting an alcoholic beverage. Musical instruments, flutes made from the leg bones of red-crowned cranes, with five, six and seven note scales, together with finds of paper and writing, exemplify society with a high degree of all round sophistication. There were also domestic sheep, goats, cattle and, of course, a range of dogs for herding, hunting and security.

As the climate gradually warmed, man drifted northwards with his livestock, in the wake of the retreating glaciers. Dog burials have been unearthed at Skatholm, Sweden, spanning the dates between 5,250–3,700BP. This brings us to biblical times and into the compass of the earliest Chinese writings. The early Greeks, whose third century BC empire stretched east into Central Asia and India, laid the foundations of the first modern civilisation. The Greeks held their hunting and herding dogs in highest esteem. The Romans took things several stages further, as their empire swept right across Europe, Asia Minor and North Africa. A central administration created a road network, established law and order and improved all aspects of agriculture. White Mediterranean sheep and cattle were introduced to the genetically black British stock by the Belgae, a Celtic tribe from modern-day Belgium. Predating the Roman invasion, this incursion into south-east Britain brought us new breeds of hunting and herding dogs. At a later point, British-bred hounds and British-made garments were greatly prized by the aristocracy of Rome.

The Romans also developed the use of dogs in war. Large, mastiff-type dogs, already adept in the role of guardians, were now trained to fight alongside soldiers and charioteers. Not only would these dogs attack the enemy on command, they would be expected to stand their ground to faithfully protect fallen handlers. By careful and selective breeding over time, these monstrously fierce dogs became the gentle and constant companions to Medieval herdsmen and shepherds. Records tell of their guarding and driving qualities, also of an ability to handle large numbers of stock and round up any stragglers. At around three feet high at the shoulder, and some 220lbs/100kg in body weight, a present-day descendent is the docile Old English Mastiff, the largest and heaviest breed of dog in the world.

Roman annals recount that the inhabitants of Wales had no concept of money, measuring wealth only in cattle. By 942AD, Hywel Dda (Hywel the Good) had unified much of Wales and codified their long-existing laws. Extant documentation from the 13th and 14th centuries, in Latin and Welsh, give precise details of this early legislation and noted the modifications made over time.

Society was divided into just three strata, the top level composed of the *bonheddwyr*, or landholders, the all-important owners of livestock. Not only were herding dogs fully protected by Welsh statute, a working dog was given an equal value to that of an ox.

Using a different format, the story of Irish dogs is very much set in stone, megaliths having been raised on the landscape by farming communities around 5,000BP. Records have been sculpted in letters of the ancient ogham alphabet, and carved in animal images on standing stones, illustrating the Irish veneration of their dogs. After Greek and Latin, the written language of Ireland is listed as the third oldest, and there are many later, written accounts of the prowess of herding, guarding and hunting dogs from the Emerald Isle.

In mediaeval England we turn to architecture. Henry VII and Henry VIII were great benefactors of King's College Chapel, Cambridge, finishing the work started in 1446 by their immediate predecessor. The magnificent late 15th and early 16th century stained-glass windows are mostly the work of Flemish artists. In window number one there is a sheepdog, complete with a heavy spiked collar, keeping watch. The throat would require extra protection during any skirmish with marauding predators, especially wolves. An east window, dated 1792, in the south aisle of St George's Chapel, Windsor, shows a moonlit pastoral scene of angels, shepherds, sheep and a sheepdog. *A Treatise on English Dogges*, 1576, written by Johannes Caius, contains a fund of information. The court physician in turn to Edward VI, Bloody Mary and Elizabeth I, Caius is considered by many to be the founder of zoological science.

Caius describes how the shepherd, by means of pointing, shouting and whistling, has his dogs bring the sheep to where he wants them to be. Also, with little effort on his part, the shepherd's dog will take the sheep to the place required. The doctor details the role of the Comforter Shepherd's Dog Mastiff in protecting both man and sheep. Alternatively known as a Ban Dog, from the Old German *ban* and Old Norse *bann*, meaning to command in the military sense, this is the precursor of the much more placid Old English Mastiff. Caius records that as he travelled northwards, the ears of dogs became noticeably smaller and placed closer to the head. This is simply an adaptation to reduce heat loss in colder climates, a trait Caius clearly observed in Iceland and Scandinavia.

Taxes on dogs had been imposed in Britain since Saxon times, to raise revenue for the Crown. There had also been restrictions on dogs of certain types, a step to limit the poaching of royal game. Herding dogs had always been exempt from such regulations. Restored to the throne of England in 1660, and desperately short of money, Charles II brought in a dog tax. Again, dogs for herding animals, along with those for controlling vermin and the leading of blind

people, were deemed to be excused. Any dog not liable to the tax would be docked at the tail, known as being cur-tailed.

In 1811, Thomas Bewick refers to a Cur as a distinct type of working dog, chiefly used as a cattle-droving dog. These were noted as being stronger and more fierce than the dogs used by shepherds, many whelped with short tails, naturally cur-tailed. *Kurre* is a Swedish term for a dog. In Bewick's time, more than 120,000 head of Scottish cattle were being driven annually into England. Bewick's *A General History of British Quadrupeds*, published in 1790, was enhanced by his own woodcut engravings. As well as his signature, Bewick impressed a fingerprint on his work, surely one of the first to appreciate the uniqueness of such a mark. Mrs Stewart Mackenzie, in the 1840s, travelling from the south of England to Ross-shire each autumn, remarked in letters to her friends and family on the number of collies, all quite unaccompanied, making their way steadily northward. Their owners, at the end of the drove, would stay on in the south, earning extra money at harvest work, whilst the dogs returned home alone.

George R Jess, another English dog enthusiast, published *History of the British Dog* in 1866. Mention is made of the worth, ancient laws and many charters appertaining to the dogs of shepherds and cattle drovers. Up and down the land, dogs were busy driving cattle, sheep, geese and turkeys to market. Emerging railway companies actually not employed collie dogs, as in upland areas it was essential to keep the tracks clear of marauding sheep.

Scotland can certainly lay claim to being the birth place of the most famous of all sheepdogs, the Border Collie. Renowned throughout the world, Border Collies feature in the works of several notable Scottish writers. Two, Robert Burns and James Hogg, had personal experience of working with sheepdogs and fully appreciated their true worth. The poems of Burns and the prose of Hogg are enriched with references to their favourite sheepdogs. The formation of the International Sheep Dog Society (ISDS), in 1906, set out to bring a degree of organisation to the plethora of breeds, strains and bloodlines in the world of herding dogs. Irrespective of size, colour or texture of coat, classification was simply as Working Sheepdog or Bearded Collie. The emphasis was totally on working ability. Mr Reid, a Scots born secretary of the ISDS, coined the term Border Collie in deference to this strain rapidly becoming numerically dominant, and originating in the Cheviot Hills.

The Border Collie Club of Great Britain was established in 1975 and, with a breed standard now based on beauty and not brains, was in a position to apply for Kennel Club recognition. But it was in the field of obedience and agility trials that the Border Collie rapidly proved its versatility – and complete mastery. Through the stud books of the ISDS, first published in 1955, bloodlines of registered working dogs can be traced back for more than a century. Success on the sheepdog trial field is helping the ISDS achieve its main aim – improving the working prowess of sheepdogs. Even within the Kennel Club competitions, it is only in the show ring that looks are more important than other attributes of stamina and skill. However, it is under the auspices of both organisations that the Border Collie has become ever more popular. There is a worldwide demand for British dogs.

A widespread trade in dogs began long ago with the Chinese and Phoenicians. The lasting influence of Viking transactions can be seen in present day British herding breeds, Corgi and Lancashire Heeler, dogs clearly descended from Swedish Vallhund and Norwegian Lundehund stock. Later commerce dispersed excellent working dogs from Britain to the colonies, with good and lasting effect. From imported bloodlines, a family called Smithfield developed an Australian cattle dog, now known by that name. Either by chance or design, genes from the droving dog of London's Smithfield Market were included in the mix. Alexander McNab, in the late 1800s, bred a new strain from the old Scotch Collie, itself an ancestor of the Border Collie, to work his livestock in California. About the same time, a Scottish émigré and his dog, Friday, were making a name for themselves in New Zealand. A vast tract of South Island is still known as Mackenzie Country. There is a monument to that rather infamous sheepdog at Lake Tekapo, and also a 40 cent New Zealand postage stamp with a picture of the statue. The full story will be told in the next chapter.

The Importation of Dogs Act 1901 was a concerted effort by the government to prevent the spread of rabies into the British Isles. A rash of rabies cases after World War I, caused by returning combat troops smuggling home pet dogs, was soon brought under control. Since 1923, with few exceptions, the six month period of quarantine has held the virus at bay. In the 21st century the world seems so much smaller, and the same rules no longer apply. Under the Pet Travel Scheme (2000) dogs can journey to the furthest corners of the globe. Dogs have even ventured out into space. Very few places still have full quarantine restrictions and, with the correct documentation, veterinary clearance and the necessary microchip, dogs can travel easily to and from 54 different countries and territories. This has had the advantage of facilitating the import of entirely new breeds of dog to these shores, many of them excellent workers of livestock. Whether they will make up for the lost inherent qualities of extinct native breeds of sheepdogs and collies, featured so vividly in past records, only time will tell.

Shepherd's Tales

WHENEVER ANY TWO SHEPHERDS get together stories will definitely be told. Some stories simply pass on essential information, others may be cautionary tales designed to forestall disaster. Some accounts will be true, others apocryphal; all will be highly entertaining. Whether climbing out to gather sheep from a hill, coming together at a market, show or sheepdog trial, or simply meeting in the pub, companionship and yarns will be greatly relished. A working life-time, beginning as a farm boy and finishing as a fully-fledged hill shepherd, has left me with an enormous collection of memories and stories. The one constant theme through these wide-ranging and quite diverse tales – the shepherd's dog.

As befits a profession, shepherds have their own patron saint, St Cuthbert. He was a Border Scot, born in 634AD, to a wealthy Anglo-Saxon family in the upper reaches of Lauderdale. In his early years Cuthbert herded sheep on the Lammermuir Hills, his dogs at his side. St Cuthbert's Way is a long-distance walk later established by pilgrims making their way from his home cloisters of Melrose Abbey to the seat of his see as bishop of Lindisfarne. With the gifts of prophecy and healing, together with extraordinary charisma, Cuthbert had the ear of kings as well as the people. After the Synod of Whitby, 664AD, Cuthbert encouraged Roman Catholicism to come to Scotland.

Dogs, however, have two patron saints: one to care for normal and sane dogs, the other responsible for completely mad dogs. St Hubert (died 727AD) had a vision of the crucifixion whilst out hunt-ing on Good Friday, and became a man of the cloth. Eventually installed as bishop of Maastricht, then bishop of Liège, Hubert never lost his enthusiasm for the hunt or love of dogs. Sane ones, of course. Mad dogs should be taken to drink at the well of St Sithney (Sezni), near Helston, in Cornwall. It is said that, when he had been offered the role as patron saint of girls, the thought of dealing with the endless requests for husbands and fine clothes, Sithney had opted to take on mad dog duties instead. His Feast Day is 4 August.

Very few people will never have heard of Lassie. After a career taking in seven Hollywood feature films and 19 years worth of television series, the adventures of the golden-coated Rough Collie are known throughout the world. The original story was written by Eric Knight, and is based on a true incident from World War 1. On New Years Day 1915, the Royal Naval battleship *Formidable* was torpedoed off the South Devon coast. Bodies washed up at Lyme Regis were taken up and laid out in the Pilot Boat public house. The landlord's collie-type dog persisted in licking the bare feet of one of the unfortunate matelots. On further examination, the sailor was found to be still alive, undoubtedly saved by the attention of that dog.

Published in 1940, Knight's first story was entitled *Lassie Come Home*. This was a real tear-jerker, telling the tale of a wartime family who were forced by circumstances to sell their family collie. The book is set in Yorkshire, and tells of all the trials, tribulations and long journey that ensued before Lassie is finally reunited with her young master. Over in America, a handsome Rough Collie dog, called Pal, was selected to play the lead role in the film version, and did so for many years. Several of Pal's offspring reprised the role in the later televised series. Officially re-branded as his alter ego, Lassie was in great demand for public appearances, and was smart enough that nobody ever saw through the disguise. A quick learner, Lassie could really do many of her own stunts, exactly as shown on the screen.

There are countless true stories of sheepdogs making long journeys. This was told to me by Andrew Hall, who publishes the *Working Sheepdog News*. An unaccompanied collie gets on the London-bound bus in Barnsley. It settled down comfortably for the long trip to the capital. Arriving at Victoria Bus Station, the sheepdog gets off and disappears into the crowd. Just moments before the bus was due to start the return journey, the dog reappears and comes back on board. Of course, the dog alighted at Barnsley. Neither of the bus drivers had ever seen the dog before – or since.

The Americans, not to be outdone, have a story from Oregon. Bobby, a sheepdog, was lost on a family holiday to Indiana. After much searching, with no luck at all, Bobby was left to his fate. Six months later a rather bedraggled dog arrived back at his home in Silverton, an odyssey of 2,800 miles. An average of over 15 miles every day is pretty good going. That happened away back in 1923, and the town still holds an annual children's pet parade to mark the event.

Not all roving collies cover that amount of distance, but some seem to have an ulterior motive. Harvey was a ten-month-old Border Collie, living quite comfortably in a family environment at Kirknewton, not far from Edinburgh. Although hardly more than a puppy, Harvey set off alone one Saturday, to explore the outside world. Arriving at the door of a sheepdog enthusiast, just about to leave his house to spend the day attending a course of Sheepdog Handling and Management, Harvey had to come too. Also enrolled at Oatridge Agricultural College was Carol Johnston, up to that point without a dog of her own. Sometimes it pays to take a bit of time to find out exactly what kind of dog will be best suited to your needs. Taking the stray in hand, and calling him by the good working name of Gyp, there was no holding the newly-formed partnership back. Under Carol's control, Gyp proved to be a perfect pupil, friendly to everyone and a natural with sheep.

The bad news came in the evening, when Harvey's owners tracked him down. He had only wandered a mere half mile from his home, either by accident or design, we will never know for sure. However, there is a happy ending to this story. Harvey's rightful owner, Fiona Stewart, sent her young collie back to his life as Gyp, happy to continue his tuition with the Oatridge flock.

Dandy readers of a certain age will recall the adventures of another mythical sheepdog, Black Bob. First appearing in the comic in 1944, and with a career lasting 38 years, Black Bob was loved by several generations of young readers. Real cognoscenti would have avidly collected the eight Black Bob books, published between 1950 and 1965. Once again, Black Bob of comic strip fame is based on a very real Border Collie, as are some of his amazing escapades. The actual name of this wonder dog was Wattie, known throughout the Borders of Scotland as Wise Wattie.

One rather damp August morning, Wattie and his shepherd set off as usual, heading for the hills to check the sheep. They would have put up a few coveys of grouse from the heather cover, just about to burst into full purple glory, the plump birds quite unaware of the Glorious Twelfth, now only days away. To this end, the laird and his head keeper were walking the beats, taking stock of the game available for the guns. They would have also noticed how well the spring lambs were thriving, a sign of good shepherding. By the end of July, all the milk ewes should have been clipped of their wool, but there would always be one or two that hid from sight and avoided the gathering.

Unfortunately, this was one occasion when the head gamekeeper had been quick to spot a rough ewe, losing no time in pointing her out to his lordship. The shepherd had also spotted the renegade, and although the rain had cleared away, the shepherd had not brought handshears with him. She would keep her wool for today. As noon approached, the three men came together in a sheltered hollow on a high summit, to enjoy the clear views and eat their pieces. The keeper was quick to mention the roughie, to the shepherd's discomfort. This was a good opportunity to score a few points at his rival's expense. After a few more barbed comments, the shepherd sent Wattie away home to fetch his clipping breeks. These are the bib-and-brace dungarees worn at the clipping, the handshear sheathed in a special pocket on the outside of the right leg. The breeks would have been neatly rolled up and left on one of the stools used in those days when shearing sheep.

This clawed a couple of points back for the shepherd, but the keeper was confident that his opponent was bluffing. It was an impossible task, even for Wise Wattie. Time ticked by, and no sign of the dog at all. The food had been long finished, and yet the laird was hanging on to see how this situation between shepherd and keeper would end. As the shepherd became more and more concerned by the inordinate delay, the keeper was visibly growing in confidence. The day was surely his. When all seemed lost, the laird needing to move on, further down the hill, sheep were seen to be disturbed. Spy-glasses were focused on the area, and into the lenses came a Border Collie, struggling with a pair of clipping-breeks. One of the legs had become unfurled and, not to be treading on the trailing garment, Wattie was walking like a crab, sideways. A triumph for Scotland's true dog prodigy. The ewe was as quickly divested of her wool as the keeper had been of his pride.

Much has been said and written about the power of comprehension in domestic dogs. By experience I would expect my own sheepdogs to have the understanding of a seven-year-old child. Some seven year olds will be astute, others quite obtuse – exactly as you find in dogs. There are not many Watties around. The shepherd had gone down to the village, where his retired father lived, to help the old man plant up his garden. When it came to planting the cabbages, the dibble could not be found. The father was all for heeling them into the ground, but the shepherd had another idea. Wattie was dispatched back to the farm garden, to fetch the dibble from there. It will come as no surprise that Wattie duly returned with the essential tool, and the cabbages planted in the correct fashion.

Controversy continues to rage over the ability, or otherwise, of dogs to understand the actual meaning of words. Some adhere to the belief that it is entirely a matter of tone and inflection of voice. Dogs, however, can and do develop a vocabulary, sometimes quite extensive. It is not surprising that a collie like Wattie would know what clipping-breeks were, but how many times would he have encountered the word dibble? In South Wales, I frequently saw Ernie Rees throw his cap for Sheber to retrieve, usually an entertainment for visitors and local children. On one occasion I was quite impressed when Ernie sent his dog to the other end of a field to fetch his jumper. That was certainly not an everyday occurrence. A few stories will help establish just how extensive a vocabulary a well-trained dog can acquire.

Viv Billingham, one of Scotland's top sheepdog handlers, told me of a motor mechanic in the Borders with a collie trained to correctly identify a range of over 30 tools, and bring them to his master. This was especially handy when the mechanic was flat on his back, under a vehicle. There are countless tales in the same vein, without a shred of scientific evidence. But evidence there is.

A report in *National Geographic*, March 2008, featured a six-year-old Border Collie, by the name of Betsy. A case study in Vienna, Austria, showed this bitch had a proven vocabulary of 340 words. At only ten weeks she would sit on command and was soon picking up the names of a range of items, and rushing to retrieve them. In scientific tests Betsy showed herself to be competent at connecting photographs with the actual objects. She also knew 15 people by name and her repertoire continued to expand. Juliane Kaminski, a cognitive psychologist, has closely studied Betsy and Rico, a Border Collie from Germany, who shot to fame on a television show, knowing the names of some 200 toys. This research was under the auspices of the Max Planck Institute for Evolutionary Anthropology, Leipzig, concluding that the technique dogs use for word learning is identical to that of humans. Collies are particularly adept at picking up language because they are working dogs and highly motivated. Dogs' understanding of human communication has evolved through a long and close relationship with man. Any dog responding to vocal and whistle commands is actually bilingual.

I cannot stress too strongly the importance of talking to your dogs. The more you say, the greater their understanding will be. Even in what seems to be a one-off situation, a good sheepdog can often come to the rescue. I was at a neighbouring clipping in the Borders, when a half-sheared sheep broke away, cleared two fences, leapt a stone dyke and raced off to the hill. One of the shearing contractors turned to me and asked what my great dog was going to do about it. I whistled Bo away out of the back of my Land Rover, from where she had been watching proceedings, and left her to do the rest. Time passed and I was just beginning to get a bit of stick from a couple of my colleagues, when the ewe returned, wool flying out from her shoulder like the Caped Crusader.

A runaway sheep on its own is pretty straightforward for any decent sheepdog; picking out one particular sheep from a flock is an entirely different matter. Checking my 220 Glengyle hoggs on the lowland farm, where they spend their first winter, I spotted one with a length of barbed wire tangled in her long blackface fleece. Finn had easily separated her from the rest of the flock, brought the beast to hand and then took a good hold of her. Having cut the wire free from the wool, I let the hogg go, noticing a glint of more wire as she rejoined the rest. I asked my bitch to go back and get that sheep, not a task she had done before. Finn dived into the seething mass of young sheep and, just moments later, reappeared, driving the same hogg right back to my feet. As I removed the last piece of barbed wire, I'll swear that Finn had a rather sardonic look in her eye.

Working a single sheep is the most difficult task usually faced by a sheepdog. This is the reason that only at the higher echelon of sheepdog trials are dogs asked to shed and keep separate a single animal. At other trials it is normally an even split of a group of four. One of my favourite tales is about the working of an individual sheep by an exceptional dog. On the west coast of one of the islands in the Outer Hebrides, there is a crofting township standing above a church, hotel and little harbour. There is nothing further west until you get to Canada. Old Hamish, one of the crofters, had a very fine sheepdog with the yellow coat that such dogs used to have in those parts. Donald, according to Hamish, could do absolutely anything. While showing off Donald's considerable herding abilities to some passing tourists, Hamish was challenged to send his dog for a single sheep.

Realising that one Lewis Blackface sheep would pretty much look like any other of the same breed, Hamish dispatched his dog to go and bring home the township tup – in English, that would be a ram. This was a particularly young and virile beast, responsible for tending to all the ewes on every croft on that township. In fact, he was known to visit many compliant females on a lot of neighbouring ground. Seeing that this task could take Donald a wee while, and it was quite a warm day, someone suggested going down to the hotel for a little refreshment. This being the Hebrides, they soon forgot about time and they quite forgot about Donald. Until, about an hour later, the local police sergeant arrived to ask whether that would be Hamish's yellow dog, with the one lug up and the other lug down. When Hamish said that it was indeed his Donald, he was told that he had better go and rescue the priest, who was not happy at being penned up in the sheep fank at the croft.

Since their inception, at Bala, North Wales, in 1873, sheepdog trials have proved to be popular with the general public. Celtic mythology, however, can come up with a far older story of a challenge set for two of Finn McCoul's faithful hounds. McCoul, a great Scottish warrior chief, had fallen into the hands of the Picts and was being held to ransom. The first demand was for the Scots to hand over a vast amount of wealth, in the form of gold, jewels and black cattle. This was readily agreed to, because Finn's people could get them back tomorrow. The next request was for large tracts of Scots territory to be ceded to the victors. This was also granted, because the Scots could win it all back tomorrow. The third requirement was for enough slaves to weaken their opponents for years to come. These too, were handed over, because they could always be reclaimed tomorrow. The final demand, though, seemed to be a task impossible to fulfil – a parade of two of all the animals under the sun.

Bran and Sgeolan (pronounced *skilorn*), the two favourite hounds of Finn, undertook to accept this challenge and secure their master's release. A deadline had been agreed between the two parties, and a place appointed for what was to be a very grand victory parade. The two dogs disappeared into the night and not a hair of them was seen again until the designated day. Fergus, king of the Picts, was seated on his golden throne, beneath a golden canopy, on a hilltop outside his stronghold, his people all around him. With great excitement the parade began, the victorious Pictish warriors leading the way. They were followed by their Scots prisoners of war, crawling on hands and knees in complete subjugation. Next came the slaves, labouring under the enormous treasure given up to the Picts. Finally, there came the procession of animals. With great cunning, the two mice had been placed in front of the two cats. The two sheep were directly in front of the wolves and the deer were followed by two bears. By this careful arrangement, the flow of the parade of animals was assured. But it was the walking of the whales, a wonder for all to behold, that led to Finn McCoul being released.

Sheepdog trials are to be found in every part of the world where sheep are herded. The layout of the course varies from country to

country, designed to accommodate the style and working requirements expected of the dogs. Mustering sheep in Australia is not at
all the same as herding over the high ground of Scotland. Not only
are the breeds of sheep diametrically different, the herding dogs
being used are too. Even within one country there can be a wide
range of geography and sheep that have evolved to suit the ground.
Scotland alone has ten breeds of sheep, the North Country Cheviot
at one end of the spectrum and the tiny and very wild Soay sheep at
the other. In conjunction with the Scottish Wool Centre, I devised
a sheepdog trial to utilise this diversity.

The Scottish Triple Crown has everything in threes. Three of the
top handlers compete on the field, each running one dog, working
in turn with three packets of three sheep, and three different breeds
to deal with. The contrasting nature of North Country Cheviot,
Scottish Blackface and fiery Shetland sheep would be guaranteed
to put even the best sheepdogs to the test. Although held in a small
arena, the course was pretty standard but with the added element
of also loading the sheep into a trailer. Just to round things off,
each trial finished with the difficult task of taking off a single
sheep. When not battling it out with sheep, the other two competitors were both involved with judging duties. Invitations are given
out to the defending Triple Crown Champion, the current Scottish
Champion and to one wild-card challenger.

Bobby Dalziel is the only handler to have successfully defended
his Triple Crown, to be added to his International Championship
(2006) and six Scottish Championships (1986, 1992, 1995, 2004,
2009, 2011). The ladies have more than held their own with Julie
Simpson and Viv Billingham each taking home the trophy. Viv,
running her own bred, nine-year-old Tweedhope Jed, saw off a
very strong challenge from Messrs Henderson and Davidson, both
former International Supreme Champions. They even had to deal
with one of the Cheviots jumping over Jed at the shed. Viv
Billingham has published several books, detailing her knowledge
and passion for her working dogs. She is also in demand as an
instructor and has assisted me at Oatridge Agricultural College.

At every sheepdog trial, there will be somebody in the crowd who will claim to have an even better dog at home. Over the course of many years, I have only known one spectator who actually went back for his collie. The scene is a trial field in West Wales. The proceedings had come to an end, when the challenger turned up with a Welsh Collie bitch. As a few sheep were being sorted out for an extra run, the old boy announced that his dog did not actually work sheep! Taking a large, rather old-fashioned biscuit tin out of his ancient Land Rover, he turned an angry bantam hen and nine fluffy chicks onto the grass. Placing the now empty tin on its side, about 20 paces away from the birds, the farmer sent his little bitch to round them up and herd them back into the container. Tipping out the less than gruntled bantam and her brood, the trial men were challenged to emulate the performance. Several tried and a few succeeded. By which time the mother hen was really riled. Congratulations were offered, but the show was far from over.

For his next trick, the bantam and chicks were rounded up and brought gently towards the Huntley and Palmer tin. Then, quite deftly, the collie split off the hen from her youngsters and popped her into the metal box. Now the challenge had really been thrown down. Those of us who had succeeded the first time round, albeit with some difficulty, completely and utterly failed even to make the shed. Hands were extended and the dexterity of the poultry herding dog admired. But this was not a man to rest on his laurels. For a final flourish, hen and chicks were divided, the chicks penned and the furious bantam kept out. That really was a pièce de résistance!

Apart from the pleasure of good company always found at any sheepdog trial, the main objective is to fine-tune the working capability of the breed. It is certainly true to say that the better any dog is at sheepdog trials, the advantage will be best seen at home. Every aspect of a sheepdog's herding proficiency is fully tested on a trial course, and its natural facility to think and reason is enhanced.

On a lovely sunny day on the bonnie banks of Loch Lomond, amongst the spectators watching the Buchanan Sheepdog Trials, I met Professor Coppinger. On holiday from Montreal University, Professor Coppinger is a world authority on working dogs, even to the extent of handling a team of Border Collies – as fully harnessed and competitive sled-dogs.

During a long and interesting discourse on many facets of sheepdogs and collies, I was given another story about a bantam and her brood, witnessed by the professor in Hungary. The shaggy-coated Komondor is the largest Hungarian herding dog, kept as much for their protective instincts as their herding ability. Two Komondorok were put into a small pen, fenced round with wire-netting, in which a bantam-type hen and her young chicks were happily scratching. Nothing much happened, neither dogs or poultry taking any notice of each other. Then the farmer dropped a small terrier into the mix and all Hell broke loose. Before any harm could befall any of the birds, one of the big dogs stepped in to keep the yapping, hostile attacker at bay, while the second Komondor began to nose the tiny chicks to safety, out through the holes in the wire.

From a different source I was given a few tales about Hungary's best-known breed, the Puli, which first arrived in Britain around 1950. The Hungarians issued a special postage stamp to commemorate a farmer's life being saved by a pair of his Pulis, which successfully fended off a rampaging bull. The bull, and dogs in their full corded-coat glory, are shown on the stamp. The second Puli story is even more remarkable and, from a shepherd's point of view, poignant.

Every year sheep would be taken away to the high mountain pastures, staying the whole summer to graze on the verdant slopes. One such flock, gathered from all his neighbouring farms, was being tended by a single and quite elderly shepherd, assisted only by his three Puli dogs. They lived in a small wooden chalet, with nothing more to do than watch the sheep, observe nature and enjoy the solitude. Often the flock would be feeding at a distance from the hut, at which times they would all be sleeping out under the stars. This practice of transhumance has continued unbroken for at least 8,000 years, the sheep returning to their own farms for the darker months.

One year the flock returned from the mountains with only the three Pulis for company. The sheep were divided up between their rightful owners before thoughts could turn to the absent old shepherd. A search party was soon dispatched, the people being quite anxious as to their good neighbour's fate. After a thorough combing of summer grazing grounds, the body was eventually located. The shepherd had obviously been dead for quite some time. For several weeks, the dogs alone had tended the sheep but, before bringing the flock home, they had catered for their master's needs. Brought from the hut, and laid neatly on the ground around the shepherd, were his pipe, tobacco pouch, blanket, slippers, books, magazines, bottles of beer and food. Only then were the sheep gathered up for the last time that summer, and taken home.

Dogs, as we have seen, are capable of thinking and working quite independently from man. On occasion man even needs to take a step back and let his collies get on with things. In the reign of George v, two flocks of Scottish Blackface hoggs had inadvertently come together in the narrow lanes of East Anglia. The arrival of the East Union Railway in 1846 had opened up the whole area for over-wintering young sheep, distance now being no object. Soon there was a network of lines, together with countless stations at which whole flocks could be unloaded and walked to their final destination. These would usually number around the hundred mark.

Two flocks, meeting head-on, would take no time in fully mixing together. In this case, one shepherd was no more than a young boy, the other, fortunately, was older and wiser. All the sheep were herded into a nearby field and, as the two shepherds sat together in the shade of a hedgerow, the bleating animals were left entirely to their own devices. The collies soon settled themselves at the halfway point, some at one side of the field, the others lying opposite. As the older man chatted casually to the lad, who had been very upset by the unforeseen disaster, the situation began to unravel. Sheep can identify each other far more efficiently than any shepherd and they quickly began looking for their own flockmates. At first there was much random movement but, little by little, a semblance of order was restored.

Without any commands, the collies edged out into the field, gradually separating the groups congregating at either end. The next stage came when the dogs, having identified their own charges, began to rotate each group, to encourage any stragglers to head across to join the correct flock. Finally, the sheep were allowed to settle, and with no more bleating to be heard, the shepherds knew that their dogs had finished the task. Once sorted, each could go on their way. My maxim to my students is always to have faith in your dogs.

There are innumerable stories of dogs working of their own volition. In the days long before motorised transport, livestock had to be walked to and from the chartered fairs and market places. It was not unusual for newly-purchased sheep to be taken to their new home by unattended collies, driving them by the most direct route. This involved crossing open hills, passing through the resident flocks and negotiating many obstacles. One Bearded Collie bitch, driving a cut of sheep homeward from Hawick market, in the Scottish Borders, went missing. Having failed to turn up as expected, the farmer called in assistance from his neighbours and a search was to be launched.

Early the following morning, as the search party gathered together, the ewes on one of the hilltops seemed to be disturbed. In fact, that was the direction the bitch and her little flock should have been approaching. True enough, the missing sheep soon appeared, driven on steadily by the dog. The pen gate was hardly shut behind the newly-bought sheep, when the bitch further embarrassed her master by refusing to come to hand. Ignoring his increasingly heated demands, the bitch took refuge in a barn. As the irate farmer marched into the building, fully intending on administrating a degree of punishment, his dog shot out and fled back to the hill. All exhortations to return went totally disregarded. To be so humiliated in front of his peers, was too much to bear.

An old worthy, who had been the first to notice the movement of ewes on the hill, now carefully examined some loose straw in a far corner of the barn. After a few moments, he re-emerged, holding a new-born puppy in his hand. The bitch had not only whelped out on the open hill, she had somehow managed to keep control of her sheep. As the morning wore on, the new mother brought home another five puppies. Unfortunately, the last one carried in was dead. Being a Bearded Collie, and carrying a heavy coat, her master did not even realise his bitch was full of pups. Sadly, such lack of observation is still not uncommon.

Dogs can navigate with unerring precision, often covering great distances in the process. Some journeys, however, require a lot more ingenuity than others. A farmer in Lanarkshire agreed to winter hoggs from Inversnaid, on the north-east corner of Loch Lomond, providing a suitable dog was sent down with the sheep. For some reason the collie decided to go back home, quietly slipping away. To return to Inversnaid, the dog made for Gourock and awaited the ferry. Without a ticket, the sheepdog boarded the Clyde Ferry and crossed a wide arm of Atlantic to the port of Dunoon. From there the dog was faced with a 50-mile trek home, up past Loch Eck and Loch Fyne, across the 3,000ft Arrochar Alps, and around the head of Loch Lomond. The miscreant was quickly returned to his sheep-minding duties, only to abscond again. This time, whilst waiting for the ferry at Gourock, the unfortunate dog was run down and killed by a shunting railway engine.

Distances today are measured on the dashboard of the motorcar, but there is no mileometer on shanks' pony. Quite epic expeditions were shared by men and their dogs. Cattle drovers would take six weeks to walk their livestock from the markets of Central Scotland to London. Andrew MacPherson, who competed for and captained Scotland at the International Sheepdog Trials, had been prepared to hike many miles to achieve his objective. In his early years as a single man, at a time when even the remotest glen in Scotland had a resident shepherd, Andrew was due three weeks of annual holiday. This was an opportunity to take to the road with a couple of his best dogs and get onto a circuit of sheepdog trials. With the newly clipped ewes and their lambs settled back on hill until the next gathering, just for a short time, the Lord would have to be their shepherd.

Before leaving his remote homestead, tucked away in the

Highlands, the collies staying home would need to be catered for. A number of stags, shot, gralloched and dragged home off the hill-sides, would then be skinned and hung by their hocks from the rafters in the kennel. This would provide both food and exercise, the dogs being required to jump up to reach their meat. As the days went on and the food receded, the dogs had to work just a little bit harder to feed themselves. An ingenious fitness regime. Two half whisky barrels were fully filled with fresh water, and a handful of salt added to each. This was to restrict both algal bloom in the water and excess appetite in the dogs. With the dogs deeply bedded in dried bracken and the door carefully padlocked, the expedition could get underway. There were many miles in front of them.

There were trials as far west as Fort William, south to Perth, and then via Aberdeen, north to Golspie. Andrew would always be sure to win enough prize money to buy himself a new pair of shep-herd's hill boots, to replace the ones he was wearing out on the circuit. One year he had also bought a heavy tweed coat, ideal for the coming winter. Unfortunately, having slept beneath a dyke, in a field near Huntly, Andrew had gone 13 miles on the next day's walk before he remembered his new coat. On returning to the place of his overnight stay, the coat had gone. A simple lapse of memory had added an extra 26 miles to that leg of his journey. On his return home, having always at least financially broken even, the waiting dogs would be pleased to see him, and in the finest fettle for work. The shepherd and his competition dogs would have all gained valuable experience and also be in a very fit condition, full of enthusiasm and raring to return to their duties on the hill.

There is a lot to be said for good breeding. Not only are the bloodlines of Andrew MacPherson's dogs still to the fore, his son has represented and captained the English team at International Sheepdog Championships. Although a Scot, under ISDS rules, Raymond MacPherson represents the country in which he resides.

The most important concern of any farmer or shepherd is how good a dog is at working at home. There are some farmers who are not fully aware as to the capabilities and potential of a dog, and have persevered for years without one. Katie Adams, a fellow student at

Aberdeen University, managed to persuade her father that a decent dog would be more than useful with his suckler cows. Although the beasts were housed against the harsh winters of inland Aberdeenshire, calving in comparative comfort, the rest of the year the stock grazed over the fields. As the days lengthened, the cows and calves would be let out for a few hours, returning under cover for nighttime. The problem was, having tasted freedom, the cattle were rather reluctant to go back indoors. A dog might just make things a bit easier. This is where Tick was to come in and quickly prove her worth.

Bred from my own Welsh Black and Tan bloodlines, Tick was guaranteed to be strong enough to handle beef cows with calves at foot. The afternoon of the first engagement was a baptism of fire all round. It was the first time those cattle had encountered a dog, and the first time Tick had some real work to do. By the time the cows and offspring had been forced back into their night quarters, there was mud everywhere, and a great deal of it on the dog. Tick would need some serious cleaning up before being allowed back into the farmhouse. Mr Adams coaxed his mud-caked bitch to the water trough, standing at the far end of the farmyard, and gave her a thorough bath. On the second night the stock were somewhat easier to deal with, but there was just as much mud splattered around. Looking about for his hardy little bitch, Mr Adams found her already sitting in the water trough!

Teamwork between a good collie and handler can manifest itself in surprising ways. In the days before wire fencing, and with only limited dyke-enclosed areas, dogs and small boys were often invaluable. James Hogg has written much about sheep farming in the Borders of Scotland and the important role of their sheepdogs. When still at a tender age, Hogg and another young lad were to be left in charge of the newly-weaned lambs, all getting hungry and wanting to go back to mother and their own bit of hill. The ewes, once more on their hefts, soon forget about the lambs, probably grateful for the respite from constantly suckling mouths. Lambs, on the other hand, can be difficult to handle at the best of times. The boys and their dogs certainly had their work cut out.

Corralled in a steep cleuch (gully), the lambs had to be kept together for a couple of days, away from the ewes until their milk had gone. With good dogs, this was a long, drawn-out, but quite straightforward assignment. Hogg was there with Hector and Sirrah, his companion also having a pair of collies at hand, and the gloaming eventually came in around the glens. The lads needed to keep alert as these lambs were not prepared to settle, constantly bleating and looking for ways to elude the sentinel sheepdogs. The late summer night darkened and thickened – a storm was definitely brewing.

The tempest broke upon them with all the fury of a Viking raid. Lightning flashed across the sky and forked into the ground. Deafening, the thunder rolled all around them and rain lashed mercilessly down. A long way from the comfort of their beds, the boys clung to each other in sheer terror. With the coming of dawn the commotion receded into the distance, and an even greater problem faced them – the lambs had completely vanished. In fear and trepidation the boys made their way home to confess the failure of their task. Not only had they lost the lambs, they had also lost their dogs.

The whole flock would have to be gathered again and the lambs separated from their mothers a second time. But, as the shepherds made their way to the hill, dogs running around them, there were no lambs to be seen. All the ewes seemed to be grazing contentedly on their hefts. A thorough search followed, the shepherds circling the high tops and sweeping the lower landscape with spy-glasses. It was not too long before the missing lambs were sighted, the four sheepdogs still in complete control of the situation. The great Black Bob himself could not have done any better.

Not being able to see can be a handicap, but having a collie can certainly be a help. Bryn had been born blind and, as his mother had died during childbirth, had been brought up on his west Wales farm by his father and grandfather. Although in some ways restricted, Bryn was not only willing but able to pull his weight in helping out. It was a small farm, quite typical of the area, mainly dairy cows and laying hens. Self-sufficient in hay, corn and straw, there were some early potatoes grown and usually a couple of pigs being fattened up. Collecting the eggs and feeding the hens was Bryn's responsibility. The only time there would be a problem was when Bryn forgot to close the door of the hen house. The birds were quick to make a break for freedom, and difficult to get back inside. The palaver would also put them off laying for a couple of days.

When Bryn was about ten years old, a stray collie turned up at the farm. The young dog was quite prepared to settle in and adopt Bryn as his master. The older men, however, were not so keen. They had a couple of dogs about the place, neither a great deal of use. One day, the father ploughing in the top field could see a tidal wave of brown hens flooding across the farmyard. Cursing under his breath, he lifted the plough out of the ground and turned the tractor for home. Driving up to the poultry house, there was not a liberated bird to be seen. The new dog had rounded up the hens and herded them back where they belonged. The dog, now called Tyne, was allowed to stay.

Bryn was soon using Tyne to bring the cows in for their twice-a-day milking, and taking them back out to the fields. The dog became the eyes of the boy. A couple of years later, Bryn had surgery on just one of his eyes, bringing him a degree of vision. Now there was no holding the pair of them back. Bryn even bought some sheep for Tyne to really get to work on. An operation on the second eye was also successful and, although Bryn required pretty thick spectacles, he could see well enough. At 15 Bryn left school and, with his faithful dog, worked full-time on the farm.

Even the best dogs get old and slow down, often developing a few veterinary problems on the way. Apart from weakening kidneys, Tyne remained quite bright, although Bryn had to redirect his dog on the odd occasion, sending him back for overlooked stock. Six-monthly visits to the vet kept things ticking along nicely. I happened to be visiting the farm at the time of Tyne's check-up and offered to drive them to the surgery. A young locum vet gave the old dog a thorough examination and proclaimed Tyne to be in good shape – but just how long had the dog been totally blind?

The darkness of night-time is only temporary and the dawn

can reveal some unexpected sights. In Mackenzie Country, north of Inverness, lived the very last of the old drovers, a man who claimed to have slept more nights with frost on his back than he ever did in a feather bed. Crossing Scotland with a cut of sheep, he found a stance for the night, a field for the use of passing livestock. The only payment would be the manure the animals left behind. Having settled his sheep, of the male variety, the drover made for a nearby inn, leaving his three collies in charge. Rum rather than whisky was his tipple and, I am sure, he only intended to have a few. However, falling in to good conversation with the landlord and a few of the locals, the drover became quite ensconced. He assured the assembled company that his dogs were perfectly capable of looking after the tups for a few hours.

A couple of likely lads slipped out into the night, set on a little drink-induced mischief. Their intention was to chase the sheep out of the stance and away into the darkness. At a very late hour, the drover staggered back to sleep beneath the shelter of a stone dyke, covered only by his plaid. On awakening, the drover was surprised to find only one of his trusty collies watching the sheep. Calling out for the missing pair, he was answered by human voices, feebly pleading for help. Peering over the top wall, he discovered the two boys from the inn being well guarded by two collie dogs, showing teeth at their hostage's slightest move. It would not be unexpected to find several other drovers sharing the stance, the stock kept apart by their dogs. A pair of captives was a wee bit of a surprise.

James McKenzie, all six feet and four inches of him, travelled to New Zealand to make a name for himself as a drover. In March 1855, a mob of 1,000 sheep were taken away from Two Levels sheep station by McKenzie and his dog, Friday. Unfortunately, this was entirely without the knowledge or permission of the owner. With only his one dog, McKenzie drove the sheep northward through the seemingly impossible territory of the South Island. McKenzie Pass still carries his name. A mob of this size was rather too much, and they were pursued and overtaken. By keeping their wits about them, McKenzie and his dog still managed to make their escape.

Sheep from that south-west corner of New Zealand continued to disappear on a regular basis. One of the many attributes of the black and tan marked collie was that he never made a sound. The missing sheep would be sold at Dunedin, more than 300 miles from where they started. Both McKenzie and his dog were finally apprehended and faced trial, the drover being sentenced to five years' imprisonment, the dog condemned to be shot. There were, however, many anomalies to the case. Some experts doubted that only one man and a single dog could have negotiated such a route. There were other witnesses willing to give McKenzie an alibi. The dog must have been working entirely alone, so said the court of appeal. The drover was soon pardoned and sailed to a new life in Australia. Friday escaped the bullet, a dog of that calibre was far too valuable to shoot.

There is a similar story from the Scottish Borders. A dog had the ability to go well away from his own area before stealing an entire heft of sheep. Under cover of darkness the rustled animals would be brought home and hidden. After a period of time, with their ear-marks altered to disguise their true origin, the stolen sheep would pass through one market or another. Eventually, as in all good stories, the full weight of the law caught up with the villainous pair. After a fair trial, the thieving farmer was hanged, as was the punishment for stealing sheep. The dog, too, was to meet the same fate, but somehow eluded the hangman's rope. It is whispered that it was quietly relocated.

The sheer faithfulness of collies is legendary. When 86-year-old shepherd, Joseph Tagg, went missing in the Derbyshire Peak District, his Tip stayed with her master's body until he was found. The 12-year-old bitch had to wait there for 15 weeks, living on what small animals she could catch. In Montana, Shep accompanied his master's coffin on its last journey to the local railway station, watching as his casket was loaded onto a train. For the next six years, Shep met every train to call at that little country station. That dog died in 1942, killed by a train that did not stop.

A collie in Wales sat at his master's bedside through his last, long illness. After Death came to call, the dog lay alongside the

coffin and then on top of the grave, and would not be comforted or coaxed away. As time passed, the dog was in danger of being reunited with the deceased farmer, until some free-roaming Welsh Mountain sheep strayed into the graveyard. The collie dog quickly rounded up the sheep and thereafter resumed normal service. That is exactly what sheepdogs do.

Dog Tales

THE SELFLESS BRAVERY of dogs has been well documented. In 1943, Maria Dickin, the founder of the PDSA, instigated a medal for any animal who displayed conspicuous gallantry or devotion to duty while serving any branch of the Armed Services or Civil Defence Units. There were 18 dogs, three horses, one cat and 32 pigeons recognised for their part in World War II. The cat was lauded for continuing to hunt and kill the ship's rat population, in spite of receiving battle wounds, not once but twice. More recently, three dogs were awarded a Dickin Medal for their role in the aftermath of the infamous 11 September attacks in New York, and two others were bestowed with the same honour for their work in Bosnia-Herzegovina.

Some dogs develop an attachment to property. During the Clydeside Blitz, a family had been hurriedly evacuated to the comparative safety of the country. Out of necessity, the whole family of refugees were billeted in one room, albeit the parlour, of the farmhouse. The two children, sharing the sofa as a bed, would be delighted by the regular evening visit from the resident dog, as if to wish them good night. However, this notion was ended when the hostess was overheard telling her dog that the visitors would soon be gone and his own bed available once more.

A far bigger upset of domestic harmony was encountered by Prince Llewelyn, known as the Great. Having left his infant son in the care of his faithful hound, Gelert, the Welsh warrior returned to a scene of utter chaos and carnage. Blood had been splattered everywhere, even dripping from the dog, and everything that could be overturned had been – even the baby's crib. Believing the worst, that Gelert must have killed his son and heir, Llewelyn struck down the dog on the spot. No sooner was the deed done, than the little princeling was discovered, quite unharmed, underneath his upended cot. Alongside, lay the torn and still warm carcass of a wolf. Gelert would have gladly laid down his life to defend the helpless Dafydd ap Llewelyn.

Another hound, by the name of Delta, perished in the act of protecting his charge. Found buried in the ruins of Pompeii, engulfed by ash and lava spewed out from Vesuvius in 79 AD, Delta was lying across the body of a small child. Not only was the hound's name inscribed upon his collar, but also the story of how he had previously saved the life of his master, Serverinus, three times.

Loyalty comes in various guises. After nearly a century and a half, Edinburgh still boasts to be the home of the world's most faithful dog, Greyfriars' Bobby. This Skye Terrier mutt was the companion of one John Gray, a night watchman of the old city. After Gray's demise, Bobby kept watch at his master's grave for 14 years, only leaving his post each lunchtime to be fed by a local publican. Greyfriars' Bobby, or perhaps a later substitute, died in 1872, at the suspiciously great age of 18. The grave of this dog can be seen just inside the gateway into Greyfriars Kirkyard.

Marcus Terentius Varro (116–27BC), a Roman scholar who wrote a great treatise on the agriculture of his time, highlights the role of herding dogs. Varro recounts the practice of buying flocks of sheep from furthest Umbria, a mountainous region right in the centre of Italy, and walking them all the way to the south coast. After a journey lasting many weeks, the Umbrian shepherds would have delivered their sheep to the market at Heraclea. Fulfilling the contract, the shepherds would return home but leave their sheep-dogs behind, also sold as part of the deal. The dogs, however, had other ideas and soon slipped away and headed northwards, retracing the footsteps of their old masters. Varro quotes from Saserna, another expert in this field, 'Whoever wishes to be followed by a dog should throw him a cooked frog.' Maybe a good tip, but it is something I have never actually tried. Virgil (70–19BC), a later and even more famous Roman, produced an instructive pastoral work on farming and country life. This is known as Virgil's Georgics.

The true value of working dogs was not only recognised by country folk, they had aficionados amongst the upper echelons of society. Not only did Charles II bestow his own royal name on the

Cavalier King Charles Spaniel, the breed is covered by a special, unrepealed statute. This law states that no King Charles Spaniel is to be denied entry anywhere in the land. They are even to be allowed admission into both Houses of Parliament. Approbation comes no higher.

Another tale actually relates to a dog without a tail. Sophie, a blue Australian Stumpy Tail Cattle Dog, had to swim for an estimated 12 hours after falling out of the family boat. Having survived the perils of the Pacific Ocean, off the coast of Queensland, Sophie made landfall on Keswick Island, where the three-year-old bitch had no fresh water and only lizards to feed on. From this inhospitable refuge, Sophie swam across a dangerous, half-mile passage to St Bees Island, finding both water and a better supply of food. Eventually, a full five months after hitting the water, Dave and Joan Griffiths were reunited with their dog. A display of supreme ingenuity.

Work

SHEEPDOGS AND COLLIES are all officially classified as working dogs, as recognised by Kennel Clubs around the world. Between the great many breeds included in this particular category there is an enormous range of accomplishments. Simply put, all sheepdogs are collies but not all collies are sheepdogs. Sheepdogs are predominantly bred for herding sheep, but are well able to work at quite a number of other tasks. The title of collie derives from a Celtic root, Welsh *coelio* translating as trust and Gaelic *céile* meaning a helpmate, in general terms suggesting a useful dog. Of course, collies have the innate ability to work with sheep, but their scope is very much wider. Even though there is a large degree of overlap, and the names are interchangeable, both sheepdogs and collies exhibit some important areas of individual expertise.

When it comes to herding sheep, the Border Collie reigns supreme, but only in Britain and a few other places in the world where flocks are similarly managed. On the enormous expanses of Australia, huge mobs of Merino sheep will require quite different dogs. In some cultures it is usual for the shepherd to lead his sheep, in others, such as Britain, it is the sheep that go in front of the handler. Again, the sheepdogs being used will be of the breed most suited to the task. Many other forms of livestock can be controlled by the use of working dogs. Cattle come in two main categories, dairy cows, requiring a steady dog, and beef herds, where dogs need to be a great deal more forceful. Cattle dogs work closer to their stock and all have a tendency to nip at the heels – and to be low enough to avoid any retaliation. American cattle dogs lure wild stock into the pens.

Having had the experience of gathering feral goats from several parts of Scotland, I know the value of having good strong dogs. Without suitable dogs this task would be impossible. Roaming quite wild, these goats are as flighty as mountain sheep and as stubborn as suckler cows, occasionally having the audacity to attack a dog. Even domesticated goats need firm handling. In the past, large flocks of geese and turkeys would have been walked many miles to fairs and markets. Here, too, well-trained dogs would have been absolutely essential. Dogs are sometimes used in rounding up horses and ponies, especially in places where they graze freely on unfenced land. When the resident ducks went AWOL from the Scottish Wool Centre, I spent a whole afternoon doing my Saturday sheepdog demonstrations with Bran working on a pair of donkeys.

On various parts of the planet, deer are traditionally herded with dogs. Today the Sami people of Lapland may be using skidoos to get around on, but they still rely on Samoyed dogs for herding the reindeer. At the Hill Farming Research Station at Glensaugh, at the east end of the Grampian Mountains, 100 red deer hinds are run on the estate, alongside 500 ewes and 60 suckler cows. The hinds were well used to being lured in by being offered feed, coming nicely to hand. However, on days when they were required

to come in, for the likes of blood testing, many would stay well away. As Aberdeen University shepherd, I was invited to Glensaugh to demonstrate how sheepdogs could be of benefit. Using Bo, Chris and Thane, and always keeping two dogs between the deer and perimeter stock-fence, I could demonstrate how the herd could be reasonably controlled.

Collies on the hills are not always looking for sheep, sometimes they will be searching for people. From the time of St Bernard of Aosta who, around 980AD, built refuges on the high Alpine passes, specially trained dogs were kept in the mountains to rescue snow-bound travellers. By 1660, the breed now known as the St Bernard had been developed by the monks, using selected bloodlines from the dogs of Swiss shepherds. Hills and mountains are a magnet for outdoor enthusiasts and hardly a day goes by without personnel of the Search and Rescue Dogs Association being called into action. Border Collies seem to be the dogs of choice for SARDA, renowned for the ease of training and their remarkable sense of smell.

A dog has 40 per cent more brain dedicated to olfactory purpose than any human being, well able to identify one or two tiny molecules in a trillion. Put another way, if there was just one bad apple somewhere amongst two billion barrels of apples, a trained dog would find it. Some search and rescue dogs become specialists in avalanche recovery, in one case locating a victim buried under 18 feet of snow. Bonnie, a German Shepherd Dog, made her first real find under atrocious conditions, on Kinder Scout plateau, Derbyshire Peak District. Edale Mountain Rescue set out to find two lost walkers. After a long hike and on a compass baring for Crowden Tower, Bonnie suddenly pricked up her ears and bounded into the darkness. Garbed in a high-visibility jacket, adorned with a pair of bells and a chemically-activated light, Bonnie homed in on her target, and a search lasting four and a half hours had a happy ending.

A mass public trespass on Kinder Scout, the highest of the South Derbyshire peaks (2,088ft /636km), took place on 24 April 1932. More than 400 ramblers defied a posse of armed gamekeepers. This landed several protestors in jail, but eventually led to the acceptance of unfettered access to such wild places.

In the Alpine winter of 1937/38 an avalanche site had been searched and probed several times by a team from the Swiss Army. A dog kept showing particular interest at one spot, eventually beginning to bark. After a great deal of digging, a live casualty was recovered. Four German Shepherd Dogs were then specially trained-up for the Swiss Army. In 1945, the Swiss Alpine Club began training their own dogs for search and rescue work, utilising their dogs' natural ability.

A long time ago, before modern transportation, a shepherd in Sutherland had taken a small number of his own lambs to the Christmas market at Dingwall. As his best bitch was suckling her latest litter of pups, the shepherd had driven the sheep with a couple of young dogs, able enough to do the job. The lambs and one of the young dogs sold, Christmas treats were bought for his family at home: two dozen oysters, a few bottles of French wine and a flitch of ham. That would surely see them through to the New Year festivities. On the road homeward the weather rapidly worsened, flurries of snow soon becoming a steady and heavy fall. With practically zero visibility, it was only the young dog that seemed sure of the way home. Eventually, overwhelmed by cold and fatigue, the shepherd decided to dig-in for shelter and stay put until the blizzard blew itself out.

Wearing woollen tweeds and wrapped in his plaid, the shepherd settled in with his collie. Safe from the biting ferocity of the wind, and with a slow release of warmth from his garments, they had a better chance of survival. (When in contact with water each gramme of dry wool will produce 27 calories of heat.) The depth of falling snow shut out the light, but they had enough provisions with them to sustain a small siege. Entombed, not knowing day from night, Christmas completely passed them by. Meanwhile, with no thought of festivities, his wife and two small children were beside themselves with worry. On the fifth day, as they went about their daily chores, the brood bitch suddenly ran off, heading away with a definite purpose. Only 200 yards from the farmhouse, the bitch began frantically digging. The family quickly brought shovels and the shepherd and his dog were soon rescued from the depths of a snowdrift. The children belatedly received empty oyster shells for Christmas presents, and father was home in time for Hogmanay.

As part of their extensive training, SARDA dogs have to become trustworthy with livestock, especially free-roaming hill sheep. Demonstrating with my dogs at Oldham, I was followed into the arena by a SARDA display. It was arranged that I would leave the show ring by driving my demonstration sheep in and out of a line of SARDA dogs, lying unattended about ten yards apart. Not one of their dogs, every one a Border Collie, even batted an eyelid. The National Search and Rescue Dog Association proudly use the head of a collie dog as their motif.

In the 1970s, the Royal National Institute for the Blind also depicted a collie, accompanied by a woman, on identity discs worn by their guide dogs. There were dogs for the leading of blind people back in the days of Charles II. We have no idea of the breeds involved, except they would have all had their tails docked to avoid the imposition of dog tax. The first guide dogs in the modern era came from two similar organisations, the Austrian War Dog Institute and the German Association for Serving Dogs. In 1923, a blind and partially paralysed German officer was a patient of a Doctor Gorlitz. As steps towards rehabilitation, doctor and patient would regularly walk around the hospital grounds, accompanied by Exelsior, the doctor's German Shepherd Dog. One day, the doctor was called away for a few minutes – patient and dog simply carried on together.

In Britain, Mr Musgrave Frankland, secretary of the National Institute for the Blind, engaged the services of a noted dog breeder, Miss ME Crooke, with a view to initiate a British guide dog service. The project was set up in 1931, at Wallasey, Cheshire, and the first successful dog was Meta, handed over to GW Lamb, a war-blinded veteran from St Dunstans. With collies being both plentiful and easy to train, initially they became the dog of choice. Collies, though, are pretty quick thinking and are not prone to hang about, so not so suitable for older or slower handlers. My Cap was matched to a young and pretty fit lady. Guide dog duties are now mostly carried out by more sedate Labradors and Retrievers.

Amongst the 370,000 registered blind people in Britain, the argument still rages around the use of guide dogs versus the famous white stick. The five percent who use a four-legged assistant to get around will always maintain that a dog is always best. *The Scottish Sun* newspaper decided to put the matter to the test with a properly organised challenge. Two fit and evenly matched young men were to take on a very familiar route in Glasgow, Mike Hughes, the Big Brother contestant with his trusty stick, and Scott Cunningham, the MBE charity campaigner depending on his dog Travis. An underground train journey was part of the quest. The dog got his man to their destination 13 minutes sooner, a 25 per cent saving in time. I rest my case.

The concept of using dogs to assist people who are deaf began in the United States. In 1979, American-born Lady Beatrice Wright and veterinary surgeon Dr Bruce Fogle devised a British scheme, based on the American system of training Hearing Ear dogs. At Crufts, in 1982, Lady Wright, in her capacity as vice-president of the Royal National Institute for the Deaf, announced the launch of a campaign for UK-trained Hearing Dogs. With the support of a popular newspaper and national television, funding from commercial and charitable sources, and the supply of essential veterinary products from Smith Kline Animal Health, the project was up and running.

Initially based at Chinnor, Oxfordshire, the organisation now has training bases in Buckinghamshire and Yorkshire, with plans for a third centre in Scotland. The first trainer to be appointed was Tony Blunt, an experienced ex-police dog handler. Training a hearing dog takes 18 months, at a cost of around £10,000 a time. At a familiar noise, the dog is trained to notify the owner by first nosing and then leading to the source of the sound. In the case of a danger, after alerting the handler the dog will lie down on the floor. Hearing dogs wear a distinctive burgundy jacket with matching lead, the only evidence to the wider public that the handler is deaf. The 750 British hearing dogs in action today provide all their owners with a far greater degree of independence and bring a better level of understanding from the public at large.

Collies in the classroom has a nice ring about it, and my sheep-dogs have done their fair share of school visits. Teachers are well known for the wide range of learning-aids they introduce to their pupils, to stimulate interest or simply to relieve boredom. Reading Education Assistance Dogs (READ) began in the United States in 1999, and has been taken up in Canada, Wales and a few places in England. Apart from the novelty of having a dog in the classroom, there is a much more specific purpose for the dog being present. If a slow or poor reader is put in a quiet space, with only a non-judgmental dog listening in, the pupil completely relaxes and rapidly gains in confidence. Significant improvements have been widely recorded.

Professor Kurt Kotrschal, Vienna, observed remarkable changes in pupils, indicating a positive influence with the use of Classroom Dogs. Over-active children calmed down, whilst very reserved youngsters came out of their shells and began socially interacting. In Corpus Christi, Texas, Professor Amy Mintz has noted improvements in child growth and development at Del Mar College's Centre for Early Learning. Leopoldschule, Karlsruhe, in south-west Germany, is just one of 120 schools in the country enlisting Classroom Dogs to boost pupil performance in class and enhance social skills. Lynda Agsten found an excellent response to using dogs at her special school for handicapped children, near Dortmund.

Charlie, a small Shetland-type sheepdog living in Wales, is the Classroom Dog enrolled at Templeton Primary School. His handler, Miss Sarah Ellis, has her dog officially registered as a Therapy Dog, an essential check on ability and temperament. Mist is a proper working sheepdog in Scotland, who also visits schools. She belongs to Laura Cunningham, one of my former students, who with Angus Jardine and Neil McVicar were the 2006 winners of *One Man and his Dog*. Mist even helped a six-year-old autistic girl lose her phobia of dogs. At first Mist sent emails to the girl, saying what a good dog she was, and also sending all important pictures of herself. A school visit was arranged but, at the sight of the dog, the little girl ran away. Much later the pupil returned, carrying a bowl of water for her guest, and some pictures she had specially drawn for Mist. Although the girl fled a second time, it was not long before she returned and, for the first time in her life, was soon happily and confidently cuddling a dog. Laura sent the emails, Mist did the rest.

Based on a pilot scheme from Oregon, the Society for Companion Animal Studies has come up with an interesting variation on this theme. At the Young Offenders' Institute, Polmont, Scottish youths with behavioural problems are paired with misbehaving dogs. Working in concert, the demeanour and conduct of both groups was shown to change for the better.

The idea of Therapets first developed in the Netherlands, when a doctor noticed that the simple action of stroking a pet significantly lowered blood pressure. Further research on New York stockbrokers showed that dog-owning high-flying financiers had more stable blood pressure during stressful periods. Loyola University, Chicago, found that dog-owning patients who had joint-replacement surgery only required around half the quantity of painkillers in comparison to other patients. Warwick University backed this up by further research, noting that having a dog reduced the pain caused by breast cancer. Depression, too, can be alleviated by having access to a dog. The University of California tested this hypothesis on male AIDS patients. Those without a dog were around three times more likely to exhibit symptoms of depression. Stroking dogs is known to cut the rate of heart attacks by reducing levels of the stress-related hormones linked to coronary disease. You can also take them for walks.

Therapets are specially selected and trained animals, used to facilitate healing and rehabilitation in often acute and chronic diseases. They can also alleviate many other conditions. The University of Cincinnati has found evidence that owning a dog will benefit children suffering from allergies. Studying 636 children, born to parents with allergies, researchers found that having a dog reduced the risk of developing eczema. Dogs appeared to convey an immunological response, with up to a four-fold reduction in allergic conditions. British scientists studied a wide sample of 2,000 urban children. With only one in ten having a family dog, the researchers measured the differences in physical activity. Living with a dog not only helped the children to stay fit and active, it also reduced their long-term risk of developing obesity and diabetes.

The first report of dogs detecting cancer, specifically melanoma, was published in the *Lancet* in 1989. Medical Alert dogs rely largely on their sense of smell. This is exactly how the onset of a potentially-lethal hypoglycaemic attack in a diabetic is recognised, and a timely warning can be given by a trained dog. A great deal of research points to the fact that specially-trained dogs can actually identify the volatile organic compounds produced by cancerous cells in skin, breath and urine. French scientists have shown that dogs can accurately diagnose even the very earliest stages of prostate cancer, a disease which, every year, kills 10,000 men in Britain. Only just behind is the very aggressive non-Hodgkin's Lymphoma, accounting for some 9,000 premature deaths in the United Kingdom. Yet, by the simple expediency of owning a pet cat or dog, the risk is lowered by almost 30 per cent. It has also been found that the longer pets have been kept, the greater the protection against the disease. Living with a Medical Alert dog is just an added bonus.

The first Epilepsy Alert Dog that I became aware of was a red and white Border Collie bitch. Without any training, the dog would place herself right in front of her owner and sit down. If any attempt was made to walk on past, the collie would sit firm and defiantly growl. It did not take long before the owner realised that this was her dog issuing an early warning of an oncoming epileptic seizure. She would have 15 minutes or so to get herself to a safe place. Epilepsy is an unpleasant condition; narcolepsy is far more insidious. This is a predicament which sneaks up like an unseen assassin, and can be just as fatal. Those afflicted fall instantly and uncontrollably into a deep sleep. Specially trained Narcolepsy Alert Dogs can prevent such an unexpected episode simply by the action of licking the skin of their handler, particularly on the back of the neck. In the same manner, they can also revive an already-collapsed patient. Many stories relate to a dog licking in order to resuscitate an unconscious casualty.

A dog's saliva also has strong healing properties, the enzyme Lysozyme acting as an effective anti-bactericide. In France, around the early the 14th century, St Roch succumbed to the plague of the Black Death. It is recorded that Roch's life was undoubtedly saved by a dog that brought him food, licking his boils and weeping sores until they were perfectly healed. Screen paintings in Devon churches show St Roch, accompanied by a dog carrying a loaf of bread in its mouth. This story is celebrated every year by St Roch's Feast Day, 16 August, acknowledged in Bavaria as the birthday of all dogs.

Collies and various sheepdogs play their full part as Therapets, along with a great many other animals. They also fulfil a role as Companion Animals, especially the smaller Shetland Sheepdog. The original notion came from 15-year-old Frances Hay, who had become severely disabled. Living in India and then Australia, Frances found her dog was quite handy to have around. Taking things a stage further and adopting a rescue Belgian Sheepdog, in 1986 a proper training regime for Companion Dogs was put in place. Although Frances Hay died at the age of 40, her name and work are carried on by the National Training Centre, Oxfordshire. These dogs are trained to assist people living with a disability, and also to provide support and companionship for autistic children. Clients include those suffering from multiple sclerosis, cerebral palsy and paraplegia, all finding the services of Companion Dogs to be invaluable.

Companion Dogs carry out tasks that most of us take for granted. They will pick up a wide range of dropped items, such as keys, mobile phones, books and cutlery. Dogs are happy to take rubbish and put it into a bin. On the technical side, they can be trained to open and close curtains, switch lights on and off, change television channels, and even answer the telephone (the receiver lifted and carried to the handler). Dogs the size of collies will provide a degree of stability, both when the person is getting up out of a bed or chair, also whilst they are walking any distance, alleviating some of the downward pressure exerted on the spine. A Border Collie can actually out-pull a husky, so propelling a wheelchair containing an adult presents no problem. Above all else, the physical companionship, especially snuggled up in bed together for the night, is a service without parallel.

Up until 1967, it was a felony to injure or kill a police dog, considered a much more serious offence than straightforward animal cruelty. Constables in the reign of Henry I (1100–1135) were to be responsible for policing the Royal Court and maintain the kennels in the Royal Mews. This is the earliest suggestion of police dogs. By the Middle Ages, there are records of money being set aside by English towns and villages specifically for the upkeep of the hounds required by parish constables. Aberdeen City enlisted dogs in 1816, laying claim to having the first properly trained police dogs in Britain. Maybe even the first in the world. Ghent, in Belgium, began using police dogs for night-time patrols in 1859. The German police set up a specialist dog training unit in the 1890s, followed by the first Police Dog Trials in 1903. These were run under the auspices of the civilian German Shepherd Dog Society and proved very popular.

Both sheepdogs and collies were listed as the first dogs of choice and, along with retrievers, spaniels, a few mongrels and one Pomeranian, became authorised police dogs in London at the outbreak of World War I. In 1914, the capital had 172 constables registered as dog handlers. It was all a bit haphazard until 1945, when Surrey Police introduced a more organised dog-training regime. The following year, having clearly seen the benefits of specialised training, London Metropolitan Police bought in six young Labradors from a farmer in Yorkshire. German Shepherd Dogs made their debut in 1948, a much more forceful animal. In the aftermath of World War II, these dogs were referred to as Alsatians (an anagram of assailant), and it was not until 1977 that the Kennel Club agreed to reinstate the old name. Today, most Police Dogs in Britain are German Shepherd Dogs.

I have no idea what your average police dog would make of Striker, a Border Collie owned and trained by Francis V Gadassi. This is a dog whose record for breaking out of a locked car, by opening a window, is 11.34 seconds (1 September 2004, Quebec). Only Harry Houdini can beat that, once escaping from a pair of Scotland Yard's best handcuffs in just under five seconds.

Historically, there have been Dogs of War since the days of Greece and Rome. In the two World Wars, some 25,000 German Shepherd Dogs were killed in action. Other breeds of sheepdogs and collies saw military service, trained as couriers and for scouting duties. Dogs are most efficient in being alert to the presence of enemies or their booby-traps. On the battle field, collies were known to carry fresh supplies of ammunition and urgently needed medical packs, often under heavy fire. Dogs could also identify still-living casualties from amongst the dead, and locate obscured cadavers. Twenty-first century army dogs are used to guard bases, track down terrorists and physically attack the enemy. The elite US Army Seals have selected a few of their Malinois (Belgian) Shepherd Dogs to have their teeth tipped with titanium, enabling them to bite right through body armour.

The Dicken Medal, the VC for animals, was awarded to Rob, a Border Collie, in 1945. This amazing dog was parachuted into Occupied Europe several times to assist the Resistance fighters. On one occasion, the Resistance put a dead farm dog to good use. Stuffed with high-explosives, the carcass was floated onto the waters of a busy canal. It was not long before the dead dog was being sucked down, as water rushed through a sluice to equalise water levels. A simple pressure-operated detonator triggered an explosion that blew the lock gates to smithereens, completely disabling the entire canal.

In 1942, the war-time government established the Ministry of Aircraft Production Guard Dog School, at Woodford, Gloucester-shire, two years later becoming part of the RAF Police Dog Unit. Roy 2808, an RAF dog conscript from Scotland, received a Certifi-cate of Commendation for his war service. This German Shepherd Dog saw active service in Europe and the Far East. Returned to his owners after the war, with half his right ear missing, Roy became a regular Police Dog in West Lothian. Having enjoyed a lifetime of adventure, Roy died in his sleep at the age of 18.

In 1949, for the first time, the RAF Police Dog Demonstration Team entertained the audience at the Royal Tournament. In demand, touring throughout the world, the public are able to see how valu-able these dogs are in finding concealed drugs, explosives and other contraband, and even in identifying the smugglers. Since 1971, dogs from the RAF have been on loan for duty to HM Revenue and Customs, now part of the UK Border Agency. Nationwide, more than a hundred dogs are currently in service.

Dogs are now specially trained, in about eight weeks, by the Metropolitan Police Dog Unit. Initially used to sniff out cannabis, training quickly evolved to locate harder drugs, tobacco, illegal imports of animal products and even cash. Recent finds have included caviar, scorpions, sea horses, alligator heads, illicit Chinese medicines and CS spray. In a single year, HM Revenue and Customs Dogs helped to seize 1,434kg of class A drugs and £10.7m in cash.

Fire brigades throughout the land are spending less time attending to conflagration and more time dealing with accidents and other emergencies. Urban Search and Rescue Dogs work along with their handlers, looking for a range of possible casualties. On 11 May 2004, a plastics factory in Glasgow exploded; a four story building reduced to rubble. Four SAR dogs, based at the fire station in Aberfoyle, helped in the recovery of seven live victims and nine bodies. Dogs involved in rubble-searches wear specially-designed, protective footwear. Herding dogs are very adept at air-scenting, also having a keen scent memory. They usually have plenty of material to work on, humans shedding 40,000 smelly skin cells every minute. The Journal of Forensic Anthropology reports on work at the University of Alberta, proving elite Cadaver Dogs even detect bodies well covered by water.

These days more and more fires seem to be started deliberately and, to this end, a new class of forensic dog is being developed – the Arson Dog. Accelerant detection dogs will be a great asset to any fire brigade. In the service of man, the nose of a dog is simply without parallel.

Sometimes the paw is on the other foot, so to speak. In September 2010, Staffordshire Fire and Rescue Service were called out to recover Belle, an eight-year-old Border Collie. To their surprise, the crew found Belle had somehow become stuck, 30 feet up a chestnut tree in Cannock Chase.

Highly-skilled dog demonstration teams, from all these essential public services, are happy to show off their great prowess. The boundaries of technique and expertise continues to expand and, at the highest echelon, demonstrations can become extremely complex. Spectators can be left in no doubt as to how much less effective the handlers would be without their dogs. Public appearances also provide the teams with good opportunities for extra fundraising.

Individual dogs are frequently to be seen collecting money. Pride of place in this field must be given to a collie known as Station Jim. First appearing at Slough Station in 1894, a three-month-old bundle of fluff, Jim was soon bringing in money for the Great Western Railway Widows' and Orphans' Fund. Jim quickly learned to bark each and every time a coin dropped into the collection box strapped to his side. Mostly to be found on platform five, Jim occasionally ventured into the town. During a hospital parade through Slough, 265 coins were donated to the dog, a fair weight in cash and a good deal of barking. Suddenly taken ill, Jim died at only two years old, having raised a total of £40 (£33,300 at present value). Apart from a single gold half-sovereign and a few silver coins, the money was mostly made up in old pennies and halfpennies. After his death, a public subscription paid to have Station Jim stuffed, mounted in a glass case, and placed in his rightful place on platform five. There, after more than a century, Station Jim continues to collect money for charity.

In the dog world of light entertainment, the Border Collie rules. The first of this breed to win the Obedience Trials at Crufts was from the noted sheep-herding Mindrum line, from Northumberland. Border Collies quickly went on to dominate Agility competitions in the late 1970s, introduced at Crufts as an entertainment between main events. Later, along came Flyball and Disc Dog, two more contests in which Border Collies hold an absolutely monopoly. For those who like entertainment delivered right into their living room, television has provided another window onto the collie world. Shep and Meg both starred for many years on BBC's *Blue Peter*, alongside hosts John Noakes and Matt Baker. German viewers were enthralled by Border Collie, Rico, strutting his stuff, unerringly picking from a range of 200 toys. British audiences marvelled at the dancing footwork of Gin, a finalist in the second series of *Britain's Got Talent*. How very true.

It is still the sight of sheepdogs being put through their paces with a handful of sheep, either spectating on a trial field or being watched on television, that shows working dogs at their finest. A Scot, with his Scottish bred collie, Tweed, won the first recorded trial at Bala, North Wales, in 1873. At the International Collie Trial, held in Philadelphia, 1880, Fanny, another Scottish sheepdog, saw off the rest of the field. The 1973 inaugural World Championship, held in the USA, was won by a Scot, Raymond MacPherson MBE, with yet another Tweed. That is a century of Scotland leading the world.

Other countries came along right behind. A contest for professional shepherds took place at Cureghem, Belgium, in May 1892. In the grounds of a market, on the outskirts of Brussels, 200 Merino-Magdeburgs, a rather interesting crossbreed of lambs, were put out for the dogs in groups of ten. This strain was first developed in eastern Germany by the Fink family, who improved their native Magdeburg sheep by crossing them with Merino bloodlines from Spain. The concept of one man and his dogs competing against his peers had rapidly caught on and is now to be found wherever sheep are herded. Courses may change and styles of work radically differ but the principle is always the same – to show sheepdogs and collies of the world doing what they do best.

Breeds

THERE ARE NUMEROUS BREEDS of sheepdogs and collies throughout the world, Britain alone has more than a dozen. Although the
livestock drovers of old were among the first to avail themselves of
bloodlines different from their own, it was the invention of the
internal combustion engine that really opened up the field to new
genetic material. There have always been good stockmen who,
almost by intuition, could cross two quite different strains of dog
to good effect. Selective breeding certainly favoured some breeds,
their attributes being much sought after, a few others headed for
extinction. However, the best characteristics are always maintained,
even from breeds long gone into oblivion. Some dogs are noted for
their ability as a crossing breed, the bloodlines fully complement-
ing each other. Top of the list is the Bearded Collie, a breed of great
antiquity.

Exactly when the Beardie arrived on these shores is open to
doubt. Some see a connection to the dogs of Roman times, with
similar species to be found right across their empire. Others hold
the belief that the Anglo-Saxons brought this breed on their incursion from mainland Europe. Long valued as a herding dog, in recent
years the Bearded Collie has taken it's place on the show bench.
Standing about the same size as a Border Collie, the grey double
coat stands the Beardie apart. The outer layer is substantial, harsh
and flat, the close under coat will be soft and furry. The broad
head sports bushy eyebrows and, of course, a beard, but Beardies
of old had far less top-hair than present-day strains. Show dogs are
beginning to look more like Old English Sheepdogs.

Working Beardies are popular around the Peebles area and also
in Northumberland, the ancient stronghold of the Anglo-Saxon
settlers. Many of the Bearded Collies in the north of England are
born with a bob-tail, a distinctive trait once found in the famous
Cur Dogs of the cattle drovers. In Scotland, complete with a full tail,
this is thought to be the old Scotch Collie, or very close to it,

precursor of the Border Collie. The Smithfield Dog, extensively used by the licensed cattle drovers of the City of London, came directly from the Cur Dogs, in turn passing on characteristics to the Australian Cattle Dog. Working Beardies are extremely hardy dogs, loose-eyed, always on their feet, and with incredible powers of endurance. It makes an excellent cross with the Border Collie.

To prevent problems with the heavy coat in winter, shepherds would rub a concoction of ewes' milk butter and Stockholm tar into the hair on the chest, belly, legs and tail. Not only would this mixture stop the snow adhering to the coat, it would also kill off any unwelcome parasites. This is not the sort of treatment that Cassie, the first Bearded Collie to win Best in Show at Crufts (1989), would have ever experienced.

Mention sheepdog, and immediately a Border Collie springs to mind. As a breed, the Border Collie has undoubtedly been put together from many parts, but to very, very good effect. After the Union of the Crowns, in 1603, trade and commerce between Scotland and England began to open up, to the advantage of both. The added impetus given to the Scots cattle trade by the Act of Union, in 1707, was considerable. North of the border, small family farms with Celtic-type sheep were being replaced by shepherds and large flocks of sheep. The Highland Clearances had begun. By 1767, Border flockmasters were renting sheep-walks in Central Scotland, not only bringing with them different different breeds of sheep, but also new types of dogs.

These dogs from the Borders were adept at keeping their sheep grazing where they were supposed to be, long before the introduction of fences. I can remember sheep freely grazing in Hyde Park, London, only kept in check by a few sheepdogs. Central Park, New York, played host to sheep between the 1860s and 1930s. At both Stoke-on-Trent and Glasgow Garden

Australian Cattle Dog
(markings vary)

Festivals, my own dogs managed to keep our exhibition sheep safely on the lawns and out of the flower beds.

At one point around the beginning of the 19th century, somewhere in the Southern Uplands of Scotland, a strong-eyed sheepdog made an appearance. In complete contrast to the upright working style of the loose-eyed Scotch Collie, dogs of this new strain crouched low to the ground, approaching the sheep in a stalking manner. It was the power of the eye, an almost hypnotic stare, which caused the sheep to move, rather than sheer physical presence. Although not yet with this name, the Border Collie had arrived. In 2011, a Border Collie was sold to an anonymous overseas buyer for £6,300 ($10,270) at Skipton in North Yorkshire.

Standing around 18in/45.5cm at the shoulder, in the early days it seems that these collies were mostly black coated, with white points. The classic white ruff, a modern prerequisite, was actively selected in the first quarter of the 20th century, for a practical purpose. A dog working at a distance, under hill conditions, is far easier to pick out if it has a characteristic white collar. Through sheer domination at sheep work and trials, the range of the Border Collie has greatly expanded, at the expense of many other good herding dogs. However, the best traits of these displaced lines can be seen in the plethora of colours and coat types found in the modern breed. When breeding and only selecting for working attributes, nothing good is ever willingly lost.

The Corgi is a complete contrast to the Border Collie in many ways. These are two breeds of Welsh dogs, both of considerable antiquity. Their name derives from *coch ci*, a red dog, and both are ideally built to work cattle, being low enough to the ground to avoid being kicked. Corgis can be quite mischievous and some of the cattle dogs love to catch hold and swing on the tail of any laggardly cow. It certainly gets them moving. If done too often, bones in the tail will dislocate, atrophy will set in, and the lower section of the tail will drop off. In West Wales, this is a give-away sign of a dairy farm with working Corgi dogs. Corgis are the best of all dogs in herding geese, at one time reared in large numbers as a good source of income. Corgis would guard the birds against thieves and predators, and also herd the flocks safely to seasonal goose fairs and Michaelmas markets.

Cardigan Corgi (markings vary)

The Cardigan Corgi, with the long tail, is one of the oldest breeds in Britain. Only about a foot in height but stockily built, they weigh in at 20 – 27lbs (9 – 12kg). There is no doubt that genetic material from Scandinavian dogs has played a significant part in this breed, particularly the Lunde-hund. Not only do these dogs closely resemble each other, they exhibit the same, and rather unusual, physical adaptations. Both can fold their ears backwards, protecting the meatus (ear canal), which can be closed off at will. Flexible shoulders of the Lundehund, and the forelegs of the Cardi, enable the dogs to turn and manoeuvre when in confined spaces, as you would need in specialist wild-fowlers. Farmers living in coastal communities would find herding dogs with these traits particularly useful.

The Pembrokeshire Corgi lays claim to equal antiquity, also with Nordic roots. This line is thought to have come to Wales via the Viking territory of Normandy, introduced by Flemish immigrants a thousand years ago. More popular than the Cardiganshire Corgi, helped by royal patronage, the almost tailless Pembrokeshire is also predominantly a cattle drover. A little smaller and lighter, the ears are more pointed. Lineage can be traced to the Swedish Vallhund or Väsgötaspet which, apart from the colour of coat, is almost indistinguishable from any Corgi. The Queen always has at least four Pembrokeshire Corgis in her entourage, never far from Her

Pembroke Corgi

Majesty's feet. Corgis are known for having a lascivious nature, as many a guardsman's leg has found out.

The only English heeler breed is the Lancashire or Ormskirk Heeler, now rare and quite localised. Around Corgi size, their tail carried high, a black coat with vivid tan makings on muzzle, legs and above the eyes. No white at all, except on the Ormskirk strain. The Lancashire Heeler came to prominence at the end of the 18th century, when Liverpool was opened up as an important access point for livestock coming in from Dublin. Cattle and sheep from Ireland would be driven to Manchester and other north-west markets by these dogs. Heelers were certainly favoured by butchers, being quite prepared to face up to the wildest cow or angriest bull. No beast likes being bitten on the nose. Heelers are adept at controlling vermin and handy for a bit of poaching, too.

The Old English Sheepdog enjoys a relatively high profile, mainly thanks to a series of paint advertisements. A great big, hairy dog, whose eyes can hardly be seen, completely unsuited for hill or moorland work. Mostly blue or grey in colour, often with white markings. Also known as the Bobtail, the breed carries a specific gene for a white head. This is a strong and compact sheepdog, moving with an easy, ambling gait. Similar herding dogs were known in Europe from ancient times, this particular breed being developed in the southern half of England. In the days before enclosures, sheep had

Lancashire
Heeler

to be grazed away from the valuable growing crops, an ideal task for Bobtail dogs.

At night, the flocks of the heavy sheep kept on the chalk downland would be brought back to folds at the farm. These temporary paddocks, constructed of wicker hurdles, were moved to clean ground on a daily basis. The manure left and trampled into the ground by the overnight sheep was considered as valuable a product as their wool clip. The sizeable flocks required a large number of shepherds, and the dogs to work with them. Once the sheep had been penned up for the night, the shepherds had some free time on their hands. One pastime was for a shepherd, with his upturned crook, to defend a small wicket gate against a thrown ball of tightly-bound wool. The origin of cricket. Solitary Scottish shepherds had to amuse themselves by using the head of a cromach to knock small chuckies (stones) into a nearby rabbit hole, altogether a different game.

I have owned an Old English Sheepdog, and used her for working Scottish Blackface hill sheep. As sheep get older they can become far more secretive, hiding themselves and their lambs amongst the rocks, trees and bracken. In these circumstances any dog with a voice, barking on command, will prove useful, and my big dog had all the volume I could wish for. Corrie's sonorous tones would bring the concealed sheep out into the open, where the other sheepdogs could quickly sweep them up. This extremely hairy bitch had an affinity for liquified peat and would soon be a very antisocial creature. However, a quick swim in Loch Katrine after work would clean her up nicely. Corrie's coat certainly required a great deal of attention, but it really was worth the effort. The combing of her coat would add up to about 5lbs (2kg) a year, which was spun, plied and knitted up into hats, gloves and very hard-wearing socks.

The Rough Collie, named after the fairly substantial coat, can also be a smooth collie, where the hair is very short indeed. The two strains were separated for show purposes in 1895, which is where this magnificent looking dog really belongs. Hollywood was quick to exploit the Rough Collie's star potential, with seven Lassie films. King Edward VII and Queen Alexandria took a great interest in this breed, royal patronage making Rough Collies particularly popular.

Yellow-coated working sheepdogs used to be commonplace all along the western coastline of Britain and the east seaboard of Ireland. Displaced by the Border Collie, yellow-skinned dogs have become extremely rare. Whenever you do come across them they all have one characteristic in common, an abundant double coat. The harder top coat offers protection against low vegetation and the weather, the dense under layer provides added insulation.

The Rough Collie, and its Smooth Collie counterpart, stand proud and handsome on the show bench, but are seldom to be seen at work with livestock. The herding instinct, however, must be still there. Some years ago, when on holiday from Aberdeen University, I competed at a few sheepdog trials in Wales and regularly watched a fellow contestant and his Rough Collie going through their paces.

Another of the yellow brigade is the Shetland Sheepdog; in looks a miniature of the Rough Collie. There has been more controversy surrounding this breed of sheepdog than any other. There is no doubt that the present-day Sheltie is a 20th century version of a long-established breed. Regarded from time immemorial on the Shetland Isles as a peerie or faerie dog, the small size and light body weight made it a very useful dog. Working with wild Shetland sheep, often on rocky shores and sea-washed boulders, the agile Sheltie was truly in its element. Having taken over the shepherding duties from a Shetlander, at Tillycorthie, I soon found myself in possession of my own Shetland Sheepdog. Thankfully, the sheep were well enough mannered to yield ground in her presence, but I would not like to have been left with her as my only working dog. The very fine fibre combed-out from her undercoat was taken by a Shetland lady, to be turned into socks for her husband. As with Rough and Smooth Collies, blue merle and black and tan colours are accepted.

Wales is only a fraction of the size of Scotland, and yet has just as many sheep. The Welsh also have as many breeds of sheepdogs, plus their cattle herding Corgis. Since I began my career, away back in 1960, the number of Welsh Black and Tan Sheepdogs has alarmingly diminished. These powerfully built, handsomely marked dogs are loose-eyed and always working on their feet. Their distinctive tan eyebrows more than compensates for any lack of direct eye-power.

Anciently recorded as *Gellgi*, this is probably the oldest breed to be found in Wales.

Another attribute of Welsh Black and Tans is their unmitigated bravery. My young Rees dog, having stood his ground against a Blackface tup in full flight, picked himself out of the mud, spat out his broken front teeth, and immediately set off in quite vengeful pursuit. The tup did not get away a second time. Well-coupled dogs, they cover even the roughest of terrain with ease. Throughout my whole working career, my dogs were dominated by Welsh Black and Tan bloodlines, a policy I never once regretted.

A breed long gone, having certainly left an indelible mark on the dog world, is the Welsh Blue Collie. Unlike any other sheepdog or collie, the Welsh Blue Collie had no inclination to bring sheep towards the handler. This was purely a driving dog. Before the effect of the 1845 Railway Enclosure Act came into play, sheep freely grazed the sweet grass along the unfenced track sides. In upland areas, station masters would keep a small kennel of these dogs, whose role was to clear the railway lines of foraging sheep. There was no point in just chasing the sheep off the line, the animals had to be gathered up and driven to the next station, where they were safely penned-up. Fresh dogs would be released to clear the next section. After the train had passed by, the sheep could be let out. The first dogs would be sent ahead of a returning train, re-gathering the sheep and taking them to the pens at their own station. A specialist dog, indeed, bred down from the grey droving dogs of old. Many of the present-day blue merle sheep-dogs will be carrying bloodlines of the Welsh Blue Collie.

The Old Welsh Grey Sheepdog, so popular with the drovers who walked countless fine Welsh Black cattle to the London markets, is only just hanging on. As shaggy and grizzled as the Bearded Collie and the Cur Dog, having once come from common ancestry, they are almost subsumed by the Beardie. A small number of Old Welsh Greys are still to be found in the fastness of North Wales.

The land of the Welsh Marches is fairly benign, suitable for slightly smaller and lighter dogs. Lowland sheep are also quite a different proposition from wild, unfettered hill stock. Loose-eyed

Welsh Border Collies perfectly fit the bill. Working in-bye, they do not require the broad white collar which is a feature of their hill-working Scottish cousins. Lassie, my very first collie, was a little black-coated bitch, with white points. A great worker in her own right, but my dogs were to benefit from the infusion of blood from the much stronger Welsh Black and Tans.

It was the coming of the railways, and the introduction of motorised transport, that led to the influx of the wonderful, strong-eyed Scottish Border Collie. The first dog of this kind in Wales is said to have jumped from a train, and was adopted by a Mr Lewis, at Rhayader. I remember being told this story when I was working in Radnorshire, away back in the harsh winter of 1962.

Undoubtedly the finest all-round herding dog on the planet, the modern Border Collie obviously carries many of the best genes from other breeds. The black speckles, sported by many collies on their white parts, has come from out-crossing with gun dogs. On the other hand, the Black Labrador was saved from extinction by the Duke of Buccleuch, who introduced Border Collie blood to the breed after World War 1. This is evident in Black Labradors with longer legs or a white dot on the chest and a couple of white hairs at the tip of the tail. The fourth Duke of Gordon produced the Gordon Setter by mating his English Setter bitch to his head shepherd's big Black and Tan Sheepdog. The sheepdog had a great nose and a natural ability to point hidden game birds.

One last look at the old yellow dogs. The Welsh Hillman, although not numerous, is probably doing more work than all the other yellow sheepdogs put together. Legend says that this breed was brought from North Africa to Britain by Phoenician traders. Long legged and bare skinned, the Welsh Hillman is really handy as a cattle dog, somewhat resembling a German Shepherd Dog. Like all our yellow sheepdogs, this breed has a distinctive and quite useful double coat. Not only is the undercoat useful for spinning into warm and hard-wearing yarn, the pelt can be put to good use, too.

A crofter I knew, living on the beautiful west coast of Lewis, had the skin off one of his old yellow sheepdogs, telling me the dog had been far more use to him dead than it had ever been alive. Each summer, the cured pelt was secured in the water of the burn, running down over the machair to the Atlantic. After a number of weeks, the saturated skin was carried home and left to dry. Then, laying the hide, skin-side up, on white tablecloth, a thorough beating with a stout stick followed. When the skin was peeled back, a shimmer of gold particles could be seen, having been filtered from the burn by the undercoat of the dead dog. The Greeks used the skin of a dead sheep for the same purpose – giving rise to the mythological tales of Jason's quest for the Golden Fleece.

A baker's dozen of British sheepdogs and collies have to be set alongside a great many others worldwide. Here too, each breed will be found to be best suited to the geography, climate, and the local livestock, plus any necessary ancillary duties.

Turning to Europe, the Belgians used to have nine breeds of sheepdogs. Some years ago, by sensible rationalisation, this classification was reduced to four. The Malinois is rapidly becoming the best known, taking its name from the village of Malines; this breed is the new German Shepherd Dog. Every bit as big as its German cousin, the Malinois is appreciably lighter, so easier to handle during a parachute drop. Internationally, armed forces are recruiting Malinois. The US Army Seals took Cairo on their lightning raid on Osama Bin Laden's hideaway to patrol the perimeter while the troops went about their business. Equipped with a bullet-proof jacket, fitted with the latest camera technology, Cairo could easily bite through full body armour with his titanium-tipped teeth. Later, when meeting President Obama at the elite Seals' base, at Fort Campbell, Kentucky, the Malinois was wearing a black muzzle, colour co-ordinated with his characteristic black mask and ears.

The Belgian Groenendael Shepherd Dog is all black, a contrast in colour only from the shades of fawn of neighbouring sheepdog breeds. All natural herding dogs, they exhibit a strong instinct to protect their local environment. In the days when Europe was in a constant state of flux, the people of Belgium came to rely on their local sheepdogs for protection. Not only would the Groenendael look after the livestock, they would show a healthy suspicion of all strangers. An alert-looking dog with erect ears, the Groenendael could be mistaken for a black, long-haired German Shepherd.

Also taking its name from a village, the Laekenois was developed near Antwerp. A distinctive feature of this breed is the grizzled appearance of a reddish coat, quite rough, untidy and about two inches (6cm) in length. There is the usual black shading on the face and ears, also on the tail. Linen laid out to bleach in the surrounding fields would be well guarded by Laekenois Shepherd Dogs.

The town of Tervuren lays claim to the fourth breed of Belgian sheepdog. As with the others, the Tervuren stands about two foot tall (61cm) and also exhibits black ears and face markings. The coat is especially thick around the neck, throat and tail areas, adding an extra layer of protection in case of attack. Red, fawn or grey in colour, the Tervuren has a dark overlay, the tip of each outer hair being distinctly blackened. Granted breed status in 1959, the Tervuren has made good progress in Britain and America.

The French have a far wider range of sheepdogs. In the north, around Normandy, the tall, rangy Beauceron is a black dog with red muzzle and stockings. Harlequin or blue merle dogs sometimes appear but are not popular. It is easy to see that the Beauceron is a precursor of the Doberman Pinscher. The short, double coat accentuates the height, well over two foot (65 – 70cm), and weighing in at 70 – 100lbs (52 – 45kg). The Beauceron must have double dewclaws on the hind feet.

Descended from cattle droving dogs of the Low Countries, the Bouvier des Flandres has strong links to the French department of Nord. A strapping dog, with a course coat, broad head and prick-ears. The tail is usually docked. Colours range from black, through grey and pepper, to brindle. Powerful and upstanding, breeders are taking steps to maintaining the working abilities and hardiness of the Bouvier des Flandres. Resembles a rather untidy Giant Schnauzer.

Charlemagne and Thomas Jefferson both owned Briard dogs, developed in Northern France, between the Rivers Marne and Seine. Another large, rugged dog, coat no less than 3 inches (7cm), in any solid colour except white, chestnut and mahogany. The Briard has a noble head with distinctive beard, moustache and eyebrows. The standard encourages breeding with double dewclaws on the back feet, resembling additional toes, broadening the foot to allow the Briard to pivot into very tight turns. The French Army have historically used the Briard for sentry duties, carrying dispatches and search and rescue operations. Although quite different in appearance, the Briard and Beauceron claim to share common ancestry.

In 2005, Hollywood was searching for a particularly scruffy mutt to star in the film role of Winn-Dixie. Three purebred Picardy Shepherd Dogs crossed the Atlantic, to appear in *Because of Winn-Dixie*, a heart-warming story, fitting the bill perfectly. A medium-sized, well-muscled dog, with large prick ears and a good covering of harsh, grey or fawn hair. Very effective in herding sheep and cattle, they are equally adept at many other activities, even making movies. The Berger Picard is the oldest of French sheepdogs, brought in by the Franks in the ninth century. Two World Wars drastically devastated Picardy, in north-east France, greatly decimating the breed. Now, well on the road to recovery, there are around 3,500 Picardy Shepherd Dogs in France.

The smallest of French herding dogs, the Pyrenean Shepherd is native to the mountains of the south. Known from medieval times, the Petit Berger des Pyrénées was used primarily for herding sheep. There are two distinct strains; rough-faced, which matches the rest of the coat, and smooth-faced. The ears are traditionally cropped, but if natural they must not be carried erect. Coats are shades of fawn, brindle or grey, with or without a black mask. Pyrenean Shepherds served with distinction during World War 1, even becoming company mascots. Taken to Australia by Basque shepherds, smooth-faced Pyrenean Shepherds with blue merle markings, were one of the foundation breeds of the Australian Shepherd. In 2003, a Pyrenean Shepherd lifted the World Agility Championship for medium-sized dogs.

Each summer 100,000 sheep are traditionally moved from the valley of the River Rhône up into the high pastures of the French Alps. The Chien de Crau, a lovely black or grey dog, grizzled rather than shaggy, is the local sheepdog of choice. During the transhu-

Chien de Crau

mance movements, the dogs will keep even a very large number of sheep to the right-hand side of the public road, allowing traffic to pass with comparative ease. Taking its name from the town of St Martin de Crau, near Arles, these curly coated dogs stand 20 – 25 inches (52 – 65cm) and weigh anything from 35 – 60lbs (17 – 28kg). Some have long, hooked tails, in others the tail is best described as stumpy.

The German Shepherd Dog or Alsatian is one of the best-known dogs, renowned for its loyalty and courage. A big, strong-boned dog, ideal for police and military work, many become guide dogs for the blind. A police dog in America, deliberately ignoring a command, leapt to take a bullet meant for his handler. But they really are sheep herders, especially in their native land. Eric Halsall, of *One Man and His Dog* fame, and a great sheepdog enthusiast, saw Alsatians herding sheep in the Black Forest. In Scotland, Donald MacLeod, of Ausdale, Bonar Bridge, had a German Shepherd Dog called Whoopie, good at gathering, driving and shedding sheep, finding lost lambs and acting as a guardian at an open gateway. I was practically raised by my grandfather's Alsatian bitch and I am saddened by what some misguided breeders have done to the stance of these great dogs.

Hovawart means estate watchdog, a classic black and tan breed I encountered around Hartz, in the Black Forest. A really well-built collie with drop-ears, wavy coat and bushy tail. The tan legs are well feathered, the only white is a touch on the chest and a few hairs at the tip of the tail. If it had not been for the forest, looking at a couple of working Hovawarts, I could have been back in Wales. I was told that black and tan Hovawart dogs also come in pure yellow, both colours from antiquity.

In the Highlands of Bavaria, the farmers and cattle dealers developed the solid and black Giant Schnauzer. The impressive head has moustache, beard and bushy eyebrows. The neat, short and somewhat wiry coat, concealing an under-layer, sometimes acquires a salt and pepper appearance.

Hungary has three breeds of sheepdogs of particular interest. At 30 plus inches (77cm), the Komondor is the largest herding dog in the country, believed to be of Asiatic origin. An excellent guard dog, a Komandor will defend stock against any form of attack. With a grey skin, black nose and a long, white corded coat, a Komondor resembles a giant mop on legs. The coat can take as much as two years to fully develop, and grow to more than 10 inches (26cm). First mentioned as a breed in an Hungarian manuscript of 1544.

The Puli is a medium-size breed, also known for its coat of long, black corded, waterproof dreadlocks. Less common, the cream-coated fakó dogs have black masks and white Pulis can have blue eyes. It is claimed that the Magyars brought the Puli from Central Asia more than 1,000 years ago. Certainly, in Asia the breed has 2,000-year-old roots and there is evidence that a similar dog existed there 6,000 years ago. The Puli is a natural herder of livestock, even at home working with herds of semi-wild horses. Nomads would be prepared to pay a whole year's salary for a decent working Puli. A Mexican born Puli, Cinko Duda Csebi, took the top award at the first great show organised by the Federation Cynologique Internationale, in 1978.

From Puli to Pumi, a real cheeky-chappie of a dog. Long ago, about the time large numbers of Merino sheep were being brought into Hungary, the Puli was crossed with prick-eared German and French sheepdogs, and probably the odd terrier. From this maelstrom of mating, the Pumi arrived on the scene, an all-action bundle of fun. Standing no higher than a Shetland Sheepdog, the Pumi is available in black, grey or red, the curling medium-length coat never prone to cording. An easy-care dog with particularly strong feet. A great cattle dog, the Pumi makes an excellent watch dog and hunts down vermin for fun. With erect ears, the tips turned down, what you see is what you get!

Icelandic Sheepdog or Islenskur Fjárhundur is the island's one and only native dog. Studies have shown that this breed originated in Norway and was brought to Iceland in 874AD by Viking settlers. As the importation of animals into the country was banned in 1901, the breed has remained remarkably pure. Held in high national esteem, the Icelandic Sheepdog has also been honoured with a special issue postage stamp. Very much a spitz-type dog, typical of its Scandinavian roots, the Icelander has the look of a large Corgi, although with a different coat. They can be long or short haired, commonly white with coloured patches of black, brown or grey, carrying a dense layer of extra insulation. In the harshest of environments, these dogs can fend for themselves. No Icelandic farmer is without his native sheepdog, so essential for the protection and herding sheep and horses alike.

Exactly the same as Welsh Corgis, Norwegian Lundehunds or Puffin Dogs, the keen sense of smell of their Icelandic cousin is harnessed to hunt for nesting birds and their valuable eggs. Icelandic Sheepdogs are well used to finding sheep buried deep in snowdrifts, and they absolutely excel as search and rescue dogs. Living in such close proximity to man, the Icelandic Sheepdog has developed a very gentle nature, making it a first-class therapy and companion dog.

Ireland may well be smaller than Iceland but has more in the way of nationalised sheepdogs. The Scottish Border Collie rules the roost all over the Emerald Isle, but native dogs of great antiquity are still to be found. An Irish version of the old Black and Tan Sheepdog lingers on the west side of the country, around Galway and County Clare. As people have lived on these shores since about 550BC, the roots of these dogs may go back a long, long way. Across the country, County Wicklow lays claims to a breed of sheepdog of its own, registered with the Irish Kennel Club.

Norwegian Lundehund
(The Puffin Dog)

In common with the Black and Tan, the Wicklow Collie is a strong, loose-eyed dog, somewhat larger than a Border Collie. At one time, the Wicklow was a yellow-skinned dog, often with black points, but red merle, red and white, along with the ubiquitous black and white are also acceptable. Coats are rough and the tail is usually absent. Living up to their Gaelic name, Irish collies are indeed versatile. An Irish handler, James McGee, won the 2011 World Sheepdog Trials, with a bitch called Becca.

Italian sheepdogs are every bit as useful to their owners. A Bergamasco can be a much-capped rugby player, or a sheepdog with a 2,000 year pedigree. The Bergamo Hills are in the Alps of north Italy and this sheepdog, a little over medium sized, is well coated to withstand the harsh weather. Rather unkempt, the Bergamasco has three layers of cover. The undercoat has the usual overlay of harsher guard hairs, unusually topped by an extra woolly mantle.

Maremmas

The Maremma Sheepdog is a big dog with a thick white coat, quite rough to the touch and particularly heavy around the neck. Two to two and a half feet at the shoulder, a Maremma can weigh up to 90lbs (41kg). Descriptions of such dogs are found in Roman literature and stone sculpture. There is a classical statue in the Vatican Museum. This is a herding dog, well equipped to deal with the most dangerous of predators, even wolves. To reduce the chances of injury, Maremmas had their ears clipped and would be fitted with a roccale, a fiercely spiked iron collar.

The dog takes its name from the Maremma marshlands where sheep in their hundreds of thousands would be wintered. In Italy, transhumance was often reversed, sheep leaving their home pastures in the mountains in favour of lower ground and a kinder climate. The Maremma actually live with the sheep, entirely as members of the flock. Some pups are even suckled on milking ewes. Usually working in groups of three or four dogs, as any perceived danger approaches, the dogs will move forward to see off the threat. Ideal as a deterrent against the present-day problem of sheep rustling, the Maremma is extensively used as flock guardians in Australia, the United States and Canada.

The Norwegians of yesteryear were well travelled, always off raiding or trading, often putting down roots. Items of value would be taken with them, especially their dogs. In fact, dogs were held in such high esteem, Vikings have been found buried alongside them. It was to be hoped that their faithful hounds would follow the dead warriors into the next world. Hunting hounds and herding dogs seemed to enjoy equal status.

Bu in Norwegian means a farm, so the name Buhund is self-explanatory. About as tall as a Border Collie, the Norwegian Buhund is a classic spitz-type dog, a word derived from the Germanic for pointed. Carrying pricked ears and a curled tail, the coats are either wheaten or black. Wheaten dogs have only a little white and some have a black mask. Black Buhunds may have more white, often showing as a thin collar. When a Buhund moults, it really sheds a great deal of hair. As the name suggests, the Norwegian Buhund is a very useful dog about the farm, and clearly a close relative to the Icelandic Sheepdog.

The Lundehund or Puffin Dog is a smaller spitz type, noticeably angular and with extremely flexible joints. A contortionist of a dog, and with two extra toes on each foot, fully formed, jointed and muscled, it is ideally equipped for hunting out nesting birds. No cliff ledge is too narrow or burrow too tight. The similarity to the activities of the Cardiganshire Corgi also extends to the ability to lay back its upright ears, completely closing and protecting the auditory meatus. Mentioned as far back as 1600, the Lundehund survives as another useful general-purpose farm dog.

Larger and stronger is the wolf-coated Jämthund, a farm dog of great endurance, even to the pulling of sleds. This breed officially separated from the Elkhound in 1946, but still includes the hunting of elk as one of many attributes. The people of Jämtland claim that their dogs have been bred in that part of Norway since the last Ice Age.

A particularly brave dog, more widely known as the Bear Dog, built on a reputation for never giving ground – not even to a bear.

Portugal also puts forward a herding dog as its oldest native breed. The Estrala Mountain Dog or Cão de Serra Estrela really is a mountain of an animal, appreciably over two foot tall and weighing up to 110lbs (69cm; 49kg). The Estrela Mountain Dog exhibits all the characteristics necessary to survival in a harsh environment, size: strength, endurance, agility and an ability to live off a minimal supply of food. Coat can be long or short, both with a hard texture and yellow, fawn or grey colour. There is a distinctive black mask and shades of black throughout. The ears are carried close to the head, essential to avoid excessive heat loss in winter. Portuguese Marines have utilised the fearless power and surprising athleticism of the Estrela.

The Romanians offer up even bigger herding dogs, used to take care of sheep in the high Carpathian Mountains and towering Transylvanian Alps. The Bucovina Shepherd Dog measures an impressive 30 inches (77cm), with a thick white coat with darker patches, ears down and close to a majestic head. The Romanians also believe this to be their oldest breed, used since Roman times for protecting their flocks, herds and households in equal measure. When not on sentry duty, the Bucovina was pretty useful at hunting.

Even larger, and a contender for the biggest sheepdog in the world, is the Carpathian Shepherd Dog, tipping the scales at over 100lbs. More collie looking than the Bucovina Shepherd Dog, the rough, straight and substantial coat is either wolf-grey or fawn with a much darker saddle. Recorded in a mid-19th century article, published in the *Journal of Veterinary Science*, as a dog capable of both herding and guarding stock, farm and family.

Moving further east, into Russia, the snow-white Samoyed is the most striking member of the Spitz family. Traditionally a reindeer-herding dog of the Samoyedic people of Siberia, this strong, hard-working dog will also haul sledges. Around 20 inches (51cm) in the leg, the Samoyed has a close, soft undercoat, through which a harder, weather-resistant layer grows, standing out straight. The coat is so luxurious that it was late-19th century fur traders who first brought the Samoyed to Britain. Sometimes called the smiling dog, the Samoyed is actually a good guard dog.

The South Russian Ovcharka is not a dog you would want to meet on a dark night, especially if you were a stranger. A massive three feet tall (92cm), lean, robust and carrying six inches (15cm) of course, white hair, only the black lips and nose will be visible. This Russian breed had become established by 1790, known to be a wolf-killer and popular with the aristocracy of the land. Research has shown that the South Russian Ovcharka actually has the wolf as a direct ancestor. The bloodline comes down through the dogs of the Slavic tribes living 6,000 years ago. New genetic strains arrived in 1797, with herding dogs accompanying the Merino sheep from Spain. Flocks of 2,000 to 8,000 sheep would reach the Russian Steppe after a journey lasting two years. Imperial Russian Law Books recommended breeding with these new sheepdogs. Records relate that some 2,000 South Russian Ovcharkas were working with imported Spanish Merinos, four or five dogs for every thousand sheep.

The Spanish can upstage the Russians. The Basque people speak one of the oldest languages in the world and can show Neolithic cave paintings of ancient ancestors with their herding dogs. The present-day, yellow-skinned Basque Shepherd Dog may have a 12,000 year lineage, but still resembles a Border Collie. If, through history, the dog has not altered much, the sheep of Spain certainly have. In 711AD, when the Moors invaded the Iberian Peninsula, a tribe known as the Beni Merines came with their own North African sheep – the Merino.

Around the areas of Castile and León is another breed of sheepdog which could be mistaken for a Scottish Border Collie, the Carea Leonés. The coat may be rough or smooth and appear in the usual range of colours. However, the majority of Carea Leonés dogs are classically marked black and tans, also exhibiting the loose-eyed trait. Apart from

Basque

herding the local Churra sheep, the Carea Leonés can be found taking part in all of the usual collie activities, even sheepdog trials. In the 19th century, Shepherds from Castile emigrated to the south-west of the USA, taking their sheep and dogs with them. This is how the Carea Leonés became part of the make up of the Australian Sheepdog!

The Catalan is a dog cut from a different coat. This is very much a terrier type, full of boundless energy and always looking to please its handler. Mostly used as a no-nonsense cattle dog, the Catalan will work with sheep too, sometimes up to trial standard. The long wheaten coat carries shades of black, particularly around the ears and head. They make very good house dogs, always on the alert to warn of intruders, although most likely to lick them to death.

Merino sheep are well adapted to desert conditions, their wool insulating equally well against heat as cold. Sheepdogs working under the same conditions would benefit from having a white, heat-reflecting, coat. The pure white, mastiff-like Pyrenean Mountain Dog was ideal for that purpose. A natural guard dog, both sheep and shepherd be kept safe from bandits and wild animals. The Moors were finally driven out of Spain by the armies of Ferdinand and Isabella, in 1492, leaving a legacy of magnificent buildings, Merino sheep and the dogs to go with them.

The Swedish Vallhund or Västgötaspets is wolf-coloured relative of the Pembrokeshire Corgi, if a touch longer in the leg. Vall-hund means farm-dog and, exactly as the Corgi, used mainly to work cattle. A very long-established breed, the Vallhund was not accepted by the Swedish Kennel Club until 1943. Double coated, the dark, tight top-coat overlays a range of colour from grey to yellow.

The Anatolian Shepherd Dog is another that lives outside throughout the year, withstanding the heat of summer and biting cold of winter. Formerly a hunting dog and a combat dog of war, the Anatolian Shepherd now tends to the sheep on the high Turkish plateau. As well as guardian duties, these dogs instinctively keep the flock together. The first warning is a deep bark, followed by a deeper bark – and then will come an outright attack. To prevent damage, the ears are cropped and many dogs are fitted with a spiked protective collar. Vulnerable parts are protected by growing a much thicker coat, especially around the neck and tail. The tail is also used as a silent signal, tail down and all is well, tail up for high alert. Coat colour is mostly fawn with a characteristic black mask, but there are also white, pinto (skewbald) and brindle Anatolian Shepherd Dogs.

The Kangal dog is considered to be a national treasure of Turkey. It is also illegal to export a Kangal to any non-Turkish national. A massive dog, weighing anything up to 165lbs (80kg), a Kangal can run at 30mph (50km/h). Fossilised remains of a similar dog date back 12,000 years and records mention the breed being displayed in full fighting regalia by elite Ottoman forces. One of over 30 livestock guarding dogs of Europe and Asia, the Kangal is the only one guaranteed to kill wolves. The short, fawn double coat gives adequate protection against the elements and wolf bites. Ears are traditionally cropped and, like many similar breeds, the Kangal has the usual black mask.

Turkey officially exported Kangals to Namibia and South Africa, to protect livestock from being attacked by cheetahs. This was done under the auspices of the Cheetah Conservation Fund. Since the introduction of these Turkish dogs, the number of recorded cheetah attacks has dropped by 80 per cent, so the farmers are now content to leave the big cat alone. Everyone is happy.

From Central Turkey, the Karabash is another mastiff-type herding dog. The thick, sand coloured coat makes the Karabash Dog appear much heavier than the 150lbs (68kg) that it carries. The name translates as black head (*kara bas*), this breed also exhibiting a black mask. The Karabash claims a history going back 6,000 years, to Mesopotamia. These dogs can be left unattended for great lengths of time, quietly patrolling the perimeter of a large flock to herd back any stragglers. One Karabash will watch for danger from a high vantage point. The tail will first issue a visual signal, so as not to disturb the sheep, followed, if necessary, by a more urgent vocal alarm. As a shepherd would be expected to make up any losses to the owner, the dogs on herding duties will be of the very best.

A separate breed known as the Akbash is very much a white-headed version of the Karabash.

The history of herding dogs unfolds just by looking at the westerly drift of sheep, shepherds and dogs, from the cradle of southeast Asia, crossing the Old World. More recently, man has set off to pastures new, again taking his livestock and dogs with him, and the story continues in the New World.

There are more Welsh speakers in Argentina than in Wales. It is in Patagonia that Cymdeithas Cwn Cymreig (Welsh Sheepdog Society) will find the remnants of their old breeds. Of special interest is the bearded Old Welsh Grey, a dog noted for its prowess with the cattle of the pampas. There is an invaluable genetic pool alive and well in these herding dogs of South America.

All along the Silk Route, from China to the Caspian Sea, the Central Asian Shepherd Dog is another Ovtcharka (pronounced *uhf char ka*), meaning a sheepdog, with a long and proud history. This is a huge dog, wide in the back and deep in the chest, three foot at the withers and 225lbs on the scales (92cm; 90kg). The course coat can be up to 3in (8cm), covering a substantial insulating layer, ranging from white to cream, yellow, grey, black and red. The Central Asian Shepherd Dog can also display brindle, pinto or flecked patterns. To prevent being ripped or torn off during combat with a wolf, the ears and tail are traditionally cropped very short, an illegal practice in most countries.

The Australian Kelpie claims descent from the old Scotch Collie, parent of the Border Collie, crossed with the wild, native Dingo. The offspring of a natural sheep herder and a renowned sheep killer turned out to be a great success, the progeny taking the best attributes from both parents. Border Collie sized, the short coat comes in solid black, red or brown, often with tan markings. There are also blue and red merle Kelpies. Indefatigable workers, the stamina has been ascribed to genes from the Dingo. A Kelpie called Riley set a world record when he jumped 9ft 8in (2.95m), at Casterton, Victoria. The one mystery is why the Kelpie takes its name from a Celtic water sprite.

Registered by the Fédération Cynologique Internationale, as breed number 351, the Australian Stumpy Tail Cattle Dog is the first new breed from that corner of the world. Into the melting pot went bloodlines from the Cur Dog, Smithfield, Smooth Collie and, of course, Dingo. Eventually, out came a taller, leaner, square-bodied dog. Naturally bobtailed, from the Cur Dog, the blue merle colour scheme is preferred, although there are many red merle, red and black dogs. Most have white points and some carry tan markings. The coat is never more than medium.

There is an inherent danger in breeding from two merle coated dogs, the pattern caused by the incomplete dominance of genes for white and the colour. Any white, homozygous pups will have the likelihood of being deaf, blind and extremely bad tempered.

The Egyptian town of Armant boasts a good herding dog, also known as the Hawara. Medium size and strongly muscled, the long, shaggy coat can be black, black and tan, grey or yellow. The Armant is barrel-chested and has a long, curled tail. The arched toes and thickly padded feet are well adapted to working on the extremely rough terrain. This herding dog, also relishing protective duties, was recorded in the 15th century and was known to Emperor Napoleon.

New Zealand is the home to the famous Huntaway Sheepdog, a breed commemorated by a statue at Hunterville, North Island. The New Zealand Huntaway stands two feet tall (61cm) and weighs 40 – 65 lbs (18 – 30kg). With white markings, the black or black and tan coat is usually smooth, designed not to pick up burrs, but can be the more weather-proofed rough or grizzled. This is one very noisy dog, useful for getting into the places a man on horseback or quad bike cannot go and hunting out even the most obstinate sheep. A great yard-dog, quite prepared to run across the backs of the sheep, taking the shortest route to any trouble spot. Although mostly dependant on voice and physical presence, the Huntaway will, if necessary, nip a nose or two. New Zealand Huntaways have competed at sheepdog trials. It is a handy dog to cross with other sheepdogs, begetting a good working dog with the instincts of both parents – and a little less noise.

North America is the home of the Australian Shepherd Dog. Basque shepherds from Australia came to the south-west United States in the 19th century, bringing their Merino sheep and working dogs. The conditions they found in California were not so different.

Australian Shepherd

This medium-sized dog comes in all the usual sheepdog colours, the coat either medium or short. Registered with the FCI in 2007 as breed 342, the Australian Shepherd Dog is an amalgam of Spanish, German and Scottish bloodlines. There has to be a dash of Dingo and even claims for the inclusion of Dalmatian blood, a breed brought to Britain from Yugoslavia. The Australian Shepherd has attained a high public profile, with rodeo appearances and television exposure. Hollywood got in on the act, Walt Disney releasing the film, *Run Appaloosa Run*. Rivalling the Border Collie, this upstart breed is in constant demand for all the public service roles and every aspect of entertainment known to sheepdogs.

The Australian Shepherd, however, has an ace card under its collar, a unique technique for dealing with wild prairie cattle. A team of dogs first locate the cattle and then set to work. A few dogs act as decoys, encouraging the cattle to chase after them. Other dogs work at the rear, nipping away at the heels of the herd, the rest of the Australian Shepherd Dogs covering the flanks. At this stage, the mounted cowboys canter along behind. The decoy dogs lead the cattle into the corral, before slipping out through specially designed escape hatches. The other dogs drive the cattle home and the cowboys ride up to close the gates. That is team work at its very best. An Australian Shepherd Dog was awarded best in show at Crufts in 2006.

For people like me, enthusiasts of the old style of Black and Tan Sheepdogs, North America is the place to look. Strangely known as the English Shepherd, this big, loose-eyed dog works with a characteristic upright style. There are claims that the Romans brought their ancestors to England and that it is directly related to the Hovawart of Germany. An excellent general-purpose, do-almost-anything sheepdog, happy to sort out trespassing livestock and people, control vermin and baby-sit children. In fact, everything my Welsh Black and Tan dogs used to do for me and my family.

The McNab was developed in the mid 1800s, at Mendocino, California. Alexander McNab bred a large, smooth-skinned, black and white or red and white dog from the old Scotch Collie. Mainly a cattle dog, McNab also needed his dogs to herd sheep, llamas and horses. McNab Dogs also hunted boar and deer all along the coast of north-west California. Weighing up to 70lbs (28kg) the McNab is very agile and extremely well mannered, particularly good with small children. Looser-eyed and far less highly strung than the Scottish Border Collie, this was an alert looking dog with its pricked ears turned down at the tips. A classic example of a dog being bred for a specific purpose.

As mankind spread across the globe, his livestock and herding dogs evolved to be best suited to a wide range of conditions. Some breeds of dog developed as ward or watchdogs, others specialised at herding duties. Breeders instinctively knew exactly the character-istics they needed to make any improvements, and quite prepared to go with a complete out-cross. Genes moved freely in both direc-tions, the Russian Royal Family using Rough Collies to put stamina into their hunting Borzoi Hounds. The downside of breed societies is the fact that only pure, pedigree mating is permitted; the gene pool has been closed. Over time, bloodlines die out and genetic material is lost to the breed, always at a faster rate than new genes will naturally evolve. With our understanding of the principle of genetics, new characteristics can be easily sourced from judicious out-crossing. Since tail-docking has been banned, genes from natural bobtail dogs have already been introduced to other breeds.

Now very much into the evening of my life, I was heartened by a recent report, published in *Lancet* medical magazine. French scien-tists have been observing the benefits of the use of dogs with people affected by Alzheimer's Disease. Since 1993, researchers found that patients in regular contact with a dog were much calmer than the control group, and nursing staff prescribed significantly less in the way of sedation.

When I realised that my pension was looming on the horizon, I put a retirement plan in place – for my dogs. During the last few years on the hills above Loch Katrine, I worked with an all male team of sheepdogs. Bitches produce puppies. When I hung my cromach behind the door for the very last time, I was down to four fairly old dogs, quite content to be retired, too. Father Time took his toll, until only Clyde was left with me. By an unexpected twist of fate, my fine old Black and Tan Collie went off in the interest of someone else's domestic harmony. Using your family in lieu of proper sheepdogs usually ends in tears. On a farm near Perth, Clyde quickly disabused one particularly Bolshevik Suffolk ewe and dealt firmly with the Dorset Down tups, and Clyde had found himself a new home. Quite used to herding ducks at our sheepdog demonstrations, when Clyde caught sight of a few large, white geese, I swear his eyes lit up. With two young boys and a small flock of pedigree Suffolk sheep to play with, he was a very happy sheepdog.

Over afternoon tea in the spacious farmhouse kitchen, as Roger, Clyde's new owner, reached for his chequebook, I had the sudden realisation that this was the end of an era. A full half a century of having at least one dog at heel was coming to an end.

A few hours later, as I started the drive home, I slowed down and opened my window to say goodbye. Chained to his brand new and rather grand kennel, Clyde simply refused to even look in my direction. Loud and clear, my last dog was telling me...

That'll do!

This poem was given to me by an old worthy at Campsie Show. This sonnet neatly sums up the life of a hill shepherd, in only fourteen lines.

I've herded my hills with Old Nell at my side,
She's a useful wee beast and runs out quite wide.
The flock is of blackies with heads full of guile,
Nell never gets flustered and herds them with style.
We've hunted them high and herded them low,
Been out in the sun, the rain and the snow.
She's helped me with lambs and take off white fleeces,
And always enjoyed in sharing my pieces.
But time marches on and never stands still
And the years pass us by to steepen the hill.
Now age has caught up, Nell's getting like me,
A bit deaf in the ear and weak in the knee.
If I come back as a 'herd in my next life
I'll get a good dog, 'cause Nell is my wife.

Bibliography

Ashcroft, Patricia N, *The Border Collie* , Times Longbooks, 1965

Barrington, John, *Red Sky at Night*, Michael Joseph, 1984, Luath Press (new edition) 2013

Billingham, Viv, *One Woman and Her Dog*, Patrick Stephens, 1984

Combe, Iris, *Herding Dogs*, Faber & Faber, 1987

Drabble, Phil, *One Man and His Dog*, Michael Joseph, 1978

Haldane, ARB, *The Drove Roads of Scotland*, Birlinn, 1997

Halsall, Eric, *Sheepdogs My Faithful Friends*, Patrick Stephens, 1980

Hancock, David, *Old Working Dogs*, Shire Publications, 1998

Hart, Edward, *The Hill Shepherd*, David & Charles, 1977

Longton and Hart, *The Sheepdog, His Work and Training*, David & Charles, 1976

Mundell, Matt, *Country Diary*, Gordon Wright, 1981

Nathan, SM, *Farm Dogs*, Evans Brothers Ltd, 1964

Sutton, Catherine G, *The Observer's Book of Dogs*, Bloomsbury Books, 1984

West, Geoffrey (editor), *Black's Veterinary Dictionary*, A&C Black, 1988

Youatt, William, *The Dog*, Longman, Green & Co, 1879

Red Sky at Night

John Barrington
ISBN 978 1 908373 37 3 PBK £9.99

This fascinating insight into a shepherd's life went to the top of the UK bestseller charts on first publication. Now with this new Luath edition a new generation of readers can discover the rhythms of the seasons, spend the night on the hill and learn the mysteries of how shepherds communicate with their dogs.

Powerful and evocative... a book which brings vividly to life the landscape, the wildlife, the farm animals and the people who inhabit John's vista. He makes it easy for the reader to fall in love with both his surrounds and his commune with nature.
THE SCOTTISH FIELD

Mr Barrington is a great pleasure to read. One learns more things about the countryside from this account of one year than from a decade of 'The Archers'.
THE DAILY TELEGRAPH

Luath Press Limited
committed to publishing well written books worth reading

LUATH PRESS takes its name from Robert Burns, whose little collie Luath (Gael., swift or nimble) tripped up Jean Armour at a wedding and gave him the chance to speak to the woman who was to be his wife and the abiding love of his life. Burns called one of 'The Twa Dogs' Luath after Cuchullin's hunting dog in Ossian's *Fingal*. Luath Press was established in 1981 in the heart of Burns country, and is now based a few steps up the road from Burns' first lodgings on Edinburgh's Royal Mile.

Luath offers you distinctive writing with a hint of unexpected pleasures.

Most bookshops in the UK, the US, Canada, Australia, New Zealand and parts of Europe either carry our books in stock or can order them for you. To order direct from us, please send a £sterling cheque, postal order, international money order or your credit card details (number, address of cardholder and expiry date) to us at the address below. Please add post and packing as follows: UK – £1.00 per delivery address; overseas surface mail – £2.50 per delivery address; overseas airmail – £3.50 for the first book to each delivery address, plus £1.00 for each additional book by airmail to the same address. If your order is a gift, we will happily enclose your card or message at no extra charge.

Luath Press Limited
543/2 Castlehill
The Royal Mile
Edinburgh EH1 2ND
Scotland
Telephone: 0131 225 4326 (24 hours)
Fax: 0131 225 4324
email: sales@luath.co.uk
Website: www.luath.co.uk